CATS
& THEIR
POETS

CATS
& THEIR
POETS

INTRODUCED
& CHOSEN BY
MAURICE CRAIG

LILLIPUT
MMII

First published 2002 by
THE LILLIPUT PRESS LTD
62–63 Sitric Road, Arbour Hill,
Dublin 7, Ireland
www.lilliputpress.ie

A CIP record for this title is available from
The British Library.

10 9 8 7 6 5 4 3 2 1

ISBN 1 84351 005 7

Frontispiece and tailpiece illustrations courtesy William Geldart
The Lilliput Press receives financial assistance from An Chomhairle Ealaíon /
The Arts Council of Ireland.

Set by Marsha Swan in 11 on 13.5 Monotype Centaur
Printed by ßetaprint of Dublin, Ireland

In memory of Mephisto, Ramelek, Pyramus and Pidge,
and in celebration of Minna

CONTENTS

INTRODUCTION

The cat, as everyone knows, has a unique and complex relationship with man. Very generally admitted to our firesides, yet classified in law as *animal ferae naturae*, his place in human affections has varied, and still varies, very widely indeed.

I do believe that the essence of what happened is accurately conveyed in that magical fable of Kipling, 'The Cat that Walked By Himself'. By the end of the tale a sequence of implicit bargains has been struck, and these remain in force. There is, however, in Kipling's narrative one false note, or rather a moment in which the cloven hoof of the imperialist shows itself in a distrust of beauty and in the cult of 'manliness' which is such a marked feature of the Victorian ethic. 'Three proper men out of five', says Kipling's Man, 'will always throw things at a Cat whenever they meet him.' To this day, in many quarters, it is thought or felt to be not quite masculine to be fond of cats.

Kipling sounds, in the story, another note which, if not false, is misleading. 'I am the Cat', he makes him say, 'that walks by himself, and all places are alike to me.' But, to the cat, all places are emphatically not alike, except in the sense that there are no places which are out of bounds, nowhere, however perilous, which he is not driven by his insatiable curiosity to explore. And having found a place or places to his liking, he will return to it or to them with inexhaustible persistence and guile.

I think that Kipling was right about the first reason for the cat's reception into our houses and into our company: its therapeutic value in charming the baby by its fur and its purring and its playfulness, rather than by any more material services which it might render to its hosts. The ability to catch mice comes third in the diplomatic strategy of his campaign to secure entrance to the cave. That, I think, is how it really happened. Cats were family pets in ancient Egypt, as well as being sacred objects if not actual gods. Their utility in controlling the rodent population, though undoubtedly useful to the cultivators of cereals, is surely incidental.

'I am not a friend, and I am not a servant', says Kipling's Cat. He says it very early on in the negotiations: in fact he says it when the Woman has said that, having the Dog and the Horse, she has no need of friends or servants. The Cat takes this at face value, but he keeps his counsel. That is the text which later peoples, less civilized than the Egyptians, have found hard to swallow. Many of the poems in this book are, in effect, variations on that theme.

It may as well be said at the outset that there have been cases of close and self-giving friendship and love between cats and human beings. It must also be said, in rebuttal of the widely held belief that cats cannot be trained to do anything which they do not antecedently want to do, that they can. The detailed and entirely convincing narrative of Anthony Hippisley-Cox, who trained a troupe of ordinary domestic cats to perform reliably in the ring, is in prose and so has, alas, no place in this book. I have myself seen, on a lonely farm in Brittany, three or four young lions being taught to jump over a placidly standing sheep. Hippisley-Cox once struck one of his cats, and it went on strike for five days (*A Seat at the Circus* [1951]).

There is not a great deal of evidence that the Greek or Roman poets set as much store by their cats as by, for example, their pet sparrows or, to be more precise, the pet sparrows of their mistresses. Catullus is silent on the cause of death of Lesbia's bird. Perhaps the cat, if he were the culprit, succeeded in making himself scarce or even invisible. (If I were of a suspicious turn of mind I might speculate on whether 'Catullus' might be a diminutive of 'cattus' which was the demotic Latin for a cat. While verifying this I found a word 'catillus' which means a licker of plates ... But I digress.)

Fifteen hundred years later, John Skelton was in no doubt about who killed his sparrow Philip, and devotes much of his poem to a recital of the horrible things which he hopes will be done to the cat. During the intervening centuries all too many of these horrible things were in fact done to cats, nor did this barbarity cease, nor is it even yet extinct.

The cat, like many of the rest of us, had a thin time of it during the Middle Ages. Almost alone in those dark centuries there shines out the anonymous Irish monk, who in the monastery of Sankt Paul in Carinthia in about the eighth century, wrote the famous 'Pangur Bán' (p.3). In this incomparable poem the author draws a parallel, by no means forced or far-fetched, which every writer will recognise, between the occupation of the sedentary scribe and of his guest. 'Neither hinders the other, each of us pleased with his own art, amuses himself alone.' It was to be a long time before any such sympathetic attempt to think one's way into the cat's mind was again to be made.

Geoffrey Chaucer disposes of the cat in six rather perfunctory lines about his practical utility, with no sign of affection or of close observation, and in another, rather obscure passage (in the *Wife of Bath's Prologue*) he seems to be referring to some kind of folk-belief or superstition. Superstition, and perverted religion, are accountable for those atrocities inflicted upon the cat in the following centuries, from which, in Lytton Strachey's words, 'shuddering History averts her face'.

From near the end of the Middle Ages there is an anecdote which seems to run clean counter to what might be expected. Hakluyt relates that an Italian ship's cat was lost overboard but 'kept herself very valuantly (*sic*) above water' so that the master sent a boat manned by half a dozen men to rescue her almost half a mile from the ship. Hakluyt is surprised: 'I hardly believe they would have made such haste and meanes if any of the company had been in like peril.' Italians, he explains, value a cat as a good spaniel would be valued in England. But he suspects that the captain had a special fondness for this cat. Nearly two hundred years later Fielding records a similar incident, this time of a kitten, one of many, which, falling from the window of the captain's cabin into the water, was rescued by the boatswain who swam back holding the kitten in his mouth, to all appearance dead. But while the captain was playing backgammon with a Portuguese friar, the kitten recovered, not entirely to the satisfaction of some of the crew who believed that drowning a cat was a good way of raising a favourable wind.

With the Renaissance comes the fitful recognition of the cat as an individual being. De Bellay loved cats and, in a poem nearly three hundred lines long, celebrated the life and mourned the death of his cat Belaud. Ronsard, on the other hand, did not care for cats and said so in an acid quatrain. Montaigne, their young contemporary, supplies the classic text on which so many variations have been played in the centuries since he wrote: 'When I play with my cat, who knows whether she is amusing herself with me, or I with her?'

Sir Philip Sidney (p.6) shows some direct observation of how a cat 'may stay his lifted paw' while he is deep musing to himself. And at least Sidney hopes, or rather intends, that his cat shall have a long life. Shakespeare has very little to say about cats: Milton nothing at all. There are no cats in the King James Bible and very few dogs except those which ate Queen Jezebel (I Kings 20 v 23). According to Aubrey, Archbishop Laud was very fond of cats and imported, in 1637 or 1638, some tabby cats from Cyprus, which were sold at first for five pounds each. In time, says Aubrey, they ousted the English cats which, he says, were white with some bluish piedness. Certainly the cats have been hard at work ever since, mixing up the genes.

Thomas Flatman, a little after Milton's time, observes the behaviour of cats and draws certain analogies between theirs and ours. There was to be plenty of that later on. But while, in the early eighteenth century, the number of cat-poems begins to increase, they are still, for the most part, little more than the incidental adjuncts to a polite scheme analogous to genre-painting or conversation pieces in which cats appear simply as decorative props. They are not individualised, nor, so far, is there any exploration of their mental processes. James Thomson, one of the first to put words into the cat's mouth, (p.11) makes her (she is un-named except as 'Puss') express conventional regret at the loss of creature comforts and, we must concede, an instinctive sense of impending loss. The little girl Lisy, her owner, who is being sent away (presumably to boarding-school), makes a longer speech and dwells more on the affection between them.

John Winstanley , a Dublin poet and contemporary of Swift, takes up—unknowingly of course—the Pangur Bán theme, and in his elegy (p.9) for his (un-named) cat looks forward to W. H. Davies, two centuries later (p.43). The set-up is the same: poet and cat pursuing their respective preoccupations, with the cat providing solace or a solution to the 'writer's block'. Gray's famous cat 'the pensive Selima' (p.13) is remarkable only for two things: for observing and admiring her own reflexion (which not all cats can do) and for losing her balance and falling into a goldfish bowl.

John Jortin, a mid-century Latinist, here rendered in the translation (p.8) by Seamus O'Sullivan, most movingly has his cat, speaking from the Elysian Fields, send a message of undying devotion across the waters of the Styx.

Then there is Christopher Smart. (p.15)

What, in heaven's name, can we say about Christopher Smart? He is like a visitor from another world. He has neither predecessors nor successors (except for two twentieth century jokers who have put on his skin and capered about in it, and great fun they are: see p.95 and p.98). We are tempted to say that after Smart nothing was the same again, until we remember that nobody knew about 'My Cat Jeoffry' till it was first printed in 1939, 168 years after his death. He had written some very good poetry, which was published, but *A Song to David*, of 1763, was so good that it was left out of the collection published in 1810. Browning, however, recognized his quality and wrote that he 'pierced the screen/Twixt thing and word, lit language straight from soul'.

For Smart's observation is that of a visionary, and he spent several years in confinement as a mental patient, so that his wife and children came to Ireland to take refuge with his married sister at Mount Falcon in Co. Tipperary .

Back to the mainstream poets and their mainstream poems. Poems about cats remain scarce for the next hundred years, nor are they often of very high quality. Of the three best, two, Anna Seward (p.21) and Joanna Baillie (p.22), are women, while the third is William Cowper (p.19), not the most masculine of poets. When the great names touch on the topic they are seldom on their best form. Keats's (p.26) cat-sonnet is adequate but hardly more, while Words-worth's 'Kitten and Falling Leaves' is sentimental, twee, and goes on far too long. Landor's Cincirillo (p.25), by contrast, is acutely and lovingly observed, though with a critical eye, and vividly brought to life. But from Landor we would expect no less. Byron eschewed the cat, while Blake settled for the Tyger, nor does he appear, as far as I can tell, in Tennyson or in Browning. Although Johnson was very fond of his cat Hodge, whom he indulged in various ways, as Boswell relates, and Lear of his cat Foss, they did not put them into their poems. The cat in 'The Owl and the Pussycat' is not a real-life cat. Foss was to receive his due in our time from Charles Causley (p.97).

It is an ineluctable fact that, both in quantity and in quality, the last 150, even the last 100 years have been, in English at least, the golden age of cat-poetry. Perhaps it really began with Baudelaire, who died in 1868. He wrote three marvellous cat-poems, and of one of these I give two English versions (pp.30 & 31).

For the next hundred years two things were happening. There was an increased perception of cats as individual persons, and closer and warmer ties between particular cats and their hosts. There was more precise observation of the cat's external behaviour with, in-evitably, conjecture about his mental processes, in which the tempta-tions of anthropomorphism were not invariably resisted.

At the same time the scientific study now called ethology was making progress. Much, indeed most, of its content was mechanistic. It is the study of how animals behave and why they behave as they do, and it tends to show them as machines programmed to act and think in certain ways.

'So you think I am just a machine?' says the cat. 'Have you not read your La Mettrie?'

'I beg your pardon?'

'Julien Offrey La Mettrie. A French writer. He wrote a book 250 years ago called *L'Homme Machine*. If we are machines, so are you.'

If you want to be reassured that you are no end of a fine fellow, keep a dog. If you have a cat you will find yourself being looked at with a variety of enigmatic expressions: scrutinised, perhaps appreciated in the neutral sense of that word: evaluated, sized up. Or, more likely, sized down. 'Dogs' looks are no threat to a man's self esteem', says Fergus Allen. But the cat, the cat, is a customer of another kidney altogether. I like to believe that when my cat is looking at me with those large round eyes, and slowly lowers her eyelids till they are mere slits, she is expressing contentment and perhaps even conditional approval. But it is all guesswork. Even Desmond Morris, in his comprehensive book on *Cat-Watching*, is silent on this point except to say that, additionally to the reflex narrowing of the pupils, it reduces still further the input of light. I am not so vain as to suppose that the cat is dazzled by the beauty of my face. I prefer to think that she is, for the moment, content. More than any other animals, cats force us to consider our place in the scheme of things.

No amount of behaviourist theory will or ever can dispel the mystery and magic of the cat, especially if it is applied to us, as it must be. The progress of science, so far from dispelling the mystery, has intensified it.

This, of course, is the territory in which cat-poetry has flourished, just beyond the reach of the asymptotic approaches of scientific enquiry and affective insight.

The cat-poems of our period show variety as expected. Some express simple grief at the death of a pet, some simple acceptance of cat mortality, some dwell on the baffling complexities of cat nature. Some allude, glancingly, to an Egyptian past and hint at reincarnation, and so on.

A poem which appears to be about one thing may on closer examination turn out to be about something else. Thus, a section of Eliot's *Prufrock* (p.65) which seems to be about the weather is in fact a description of a cat, while another poem, ostensibly about lions and tigers, is a passionate love-poem addressed by an English lesbian lady to another English lesbian lady. I leave the reader the pleasure of finding this for his (or her) self.

Some poets make the cat speak. The most celebrated of all speaking cats is of course Saki's Tobermory, who inhabits the world of prose. This cat is merely a device to facilitate Saki's social comedy. There is a real cat in his story 'The Penance', and in a short essay, 'The Achievement of the Cat', he says virtually the last word on the subject. Calverley's cat (p.36) speaks, in perhaps too literary a tone for modern taste, but is nevertheless convincing in what she has to say.

Don Marquis's Mehitabel (p.49) is a special case. The account she gives of life at the bottom of the—both human and feline —social ladder is entirely believable. Though it is all in reported speech, through the agency of Archy the typewriting cockroach, and though some of it ranges back through many years of theatrical history (and even further back in another Marquis poem not given here) it rings true. If we must have fantasy (and for my money we must) I prefer this to the usual stuff about Cleopatra. The thoughts which Dorothy L. Sayers (p.69) attributes to her little cat are just such thoughts as such a cat would have on such an occasion. Pollock's cat (p.28) does not actually speak, but he plays his part in the College's business no less effectively for that. I have no doubt that there was indeed such a cat in Trinity College, Cambridge, and that he vetted incomers in just the way described in the poem.

Two pieces of ingenuity in the speaking line call for special mention: that of Heath-Stubbs (p.98) when he has Jeoffrey speak of his master Christopher, and that of Fanthorpe (p.105) who provides an illuminating footnote to the story of Odysseus.

Not all the best cat-poems are by minor poets. Hardy's 'Last Words to a Dumb Friend' (p.38) is quite generalized in that it gives no details which would not apply to almost any cat. Yet the poem as a whole is intensely individual and up to its author's best. MacNeice's 'The Death of a Cat' (p.83) tells us as much about his cat's characteristics and accomplishments as Christopher Smart's does about his, interweaving this with the poet's life in Athens with his wife and their cat, Thompson. He moralizes about his feeling rather more than Hardy does, but in many ways the two poems are comparable. Roy Fuller (p.91) in 'In memory of ... Domino' says almost nothing about the cat but much about his own feelings. The cat in Edward Thomas (p.57) was not loved, even by the poet: yet she got her tribute of a poem. Even Thomas Lynch's Grimalkin (p.116), for whom nothing good can be said except that she has gained the affection of the poet's son, has clearly got under his skin and will be replaced when the time comes, for

> All boys need practice in the arts of love
> and all boys' ageing fathers in the arts of rage.

I have my favourites among the poems in the last third of this collection, not counting those already mentioned: Gavin Ewart's 14 year old cat (p.93), Anon's 'A Cat's Conscience' (p.119), Lillington's Villanelle (p.99), Scot's Ballade (p.67), Stevie Smith's Singing Cat (p.77), Alexander Gray's aging cat (p.63), Douglas Stewart's bag-lady (p.92). And, of course, Strachey's deliciously decadent invocation (p.60).

What is most remarkable is the wide variety of response. Whether it is their caressibility, their demonstrably close kinship with the most magnificent predators in the world, their flexibility both moral and physical, as though they had no bones (whereas they have in fact 24 more than we have, all apparently made of rubber), their aesthetic sense in disposing themselves in attitudes fit to drive a sculptor to despair, their ability to come and go in utter silence, their courage when cornered, their nice judgment in knowing when to turn and flee—all these things have inspired poets to feel privileged in sharing this fragile planet with enigmatic creatures who know so much that we do not.

'There are', Shakespeare (or rather Shylock) tells us, 'some that are mad if they behold a cat.' We have already noticed Ronsard. Perhaps in his case it was merely an allergy. We are reassured to hear that Napoleon, Hitler and Ceaucescu were cat-haters: less reassured to know that T.H. (Tim) White did not care for them. He even put a nastily detailed account of the torture and murder of a cat into one of his Arthurian books. But I remember that he took great pleasure in the columnist Nathaniel Gubbins in, I think, the *News Chronicle*, who related the exploits of Katinka Pusskin, Hero-Cat of the Soviet Union. But that was at a safe distance from Co. Meath where Tim was then living. I used to think this was pure fantasy till I read, in Michael Joseph's *Cat's Company*, that 'in the winter of 1942, during the siege of Stalingrad, a cat called Mourka carried messages about enemy gun emplacements from a group of Russian soldiers to a house across the street' and found her way on to the leader-page of *The Times*. Was Mourka the brain-child of the Russian propaganda machine? Who knows?

Enough of that. There are plenty of books in which the extra-ordinary accomplishments of particular cats are circumstantially re-lated. The aim of this book is simply to explore the ways in which the cat has insinuated himself into the consciousness of poets writing in English. But I have given a very few translations which appear to deserve inclusion on their own merits; one by Baudelaire, one by Verlaine, one by Valéry, one by Guillame Apollinaire, half a poem by Heine, and Derek Mahon's version from Mallarmé.

The attentive and informed reader will be aware of the debt I owe to previous collections, notably Mona Gooden's *The Poet's Cat* (1946), Kenneth Lillington's *Nine Lives* (1977), and Francis Wheen's *The Chatto Book of Cats* (1993), and I gratefully acknowledge help from Rudy Kousbroek, Antony Farrell, Paul Keegan, Andrew Carpenter, Dorothy Molloy, Michael Solomons, Hugh Leonard, David Wheatley, Gemma Fallon and Michael Craig.

CATS
& THEIR
POETS

Anon

Translated by Kuno Meyer

PANGUR BÁN

This famous poem was written in the eighth century on a copy of St Paul's Epistles by a student at Sankt Paul Monastery, Carinthia.

I and my white Pangur
Have each his special art:
His mind is set on hunting mice,
Mine is upon my special craft.

I love to rest—better than any fame!—
With close study at my little book;
White Pangur does not envy me:
He loves his childish play.

When in our house we two are all alone—
A tale without tedium!
We have—sport never-ending!
Something to exercise our wit.

At times by feats of derring-do
A mouse sticks in his net,
While into my net there drops
A difficult problem of hard meaning.

He points his full shining eye
Against the fence of the wall:
I point my clear though feeble eye
Against the keenness of science.

He rejoices with quick leaps
When in his sharp claw sticks a mouse:

I too rejoice when I have grasped
A problem difficult and dearly loved.

Though we are thus at all times,
Neither hinders the other,
Each of us pleased with his own art
Amuses himself alone.

He is a master of the work
Which every day he does:
While I am at my own work
To bring difficulty to clearness.

Geoffrey Chaucer

THE NATURE OF THE CREATURE

Lat take a cat, and fostre him well with milk,
And tendre flesh, and make his couch of silk,
And lat him see a mous go by the wall;
Anon he weyveth milk, and flesh, and al
And every deyntee that is in that hous,
Swich appetyt hath he to ete a mous ...

from *The Maunciple's Tale*

Sir Philip Sidney

THE RAT'S STRONG FOE

I have (and long shall have) a white great nimble cat,
A king upon a mouse, a strong foe to a rat,
Fine eares, long tail he hath, with Lion's curbed clawe,
Which oft he lifteth up, and stayes his lifted pawe,
Deepe musing to himselfe, which after-mewing showes,
Till with lickt beard, his eye of fire espie his foes.

from *Arcadia*

Thomas Flatman

AN APPEAL TO CATS IN THE BUSINESS
OF LOVE

Ye cats that at midnight spit love at each other,
Who best feel the pangs of a passionate lover,
I appeal to your scratches and your tattered fur,
If the business of Love be no more than to purr.
Old Lady Grimalkin with her gooseberry eyes,
Knew something when a kitten, for why she is wise;
You find by experience, the love-fit's soon o'er,
Puss! Puss! lasts not long, but turns to *Cat-whore!*
     Men ride many miles,
     Cats tread many tiles,
  Both hazard their necks in the fray;
     Only cats, when they fall
     From a house or a wall,
  Keep their feet, mount their tails, and away!

John Jortin

Translated from the Latin by Seumas O'Sullivan

EPITAPHIUM FELIS

By weight of the wearying years, and by grievous illness
Compelled, I come at last to the Lethean lake-side;
'Have thou Elysian suns,' said Proserpina, smiling, 'Elysian
meadows.'
Nay, but if I deserve it, O kindly Queen of the silence,
Grant me this boon, one night to return to the homestead,
Home to return by night, and into the master's ear,
Whisper, 'Across the waste of the Stygian waters
Your Felis, most faithful of cats, still holds you dear.'

John Winstanley

THE POET'S LAMENTATION FOR THE LOSS OF HIS CAT, WHICH HE US'D TO CALL HIS MUSE

Oppress'd with Grief, in heavy Strains I mourn,
The Partner of my Studies from me torn:
How shall I sing? what Numbers shall I chuse?
For, in my fav'rite Cat, I've lost my Muse.
No more I feel my Mind with Raptures fir'd,
I want those Airs that Puss so oft inspir'd;
No crouding Thoughts my ready Fancy fill,
Nor Words run fluent from my easy Quill:
Yet shall my Verse deplore her cruel Fate,
And celebrate the Virtues of my *Cat*.

In Acts obscene she never took Delight,
No Catterwauls disturb'd our Sleep by Night;
Chaste as a Virgin, free from every Stain,
And neighb'ring *Cats* mew'd for her Love in vain.
She never thirsted for the *Chicken*'s Blood,
Her Teeth she only us'd to chew her Food;
Harmless as Satires which her Master writes,
A Foe to scratching, and unus'd to Bites.

She in the Study was my constant Mate,
There we together many Evenings sat.
Whene'er I felt my tow'ring Fancy fail,
I strok'd her Head, her Ears, her Back, her Tail;
And, as I strok'd, improv'd my dying Song,
From the sweet Notes of her melodious Tongue:
Her Purrs, and Mews, so evenly kept Time,
She purr'd in Metre, and she mew'd in Rhime.

But when my Dulness has too stubborn prov'd,
Nor cou'd by *Puss*'s Music be remov'd;
Oft to the well-known Volumes have I gone,
And stole a line from POPE, or ADDISON.

Oft-times, when lost amidst poetic Heat,
She, leaping on my Knee, has took her Seat;
There saw the Throes that rack'd my lab'ring Brain,
And lick'd and clawd me to myself again.
Then, Friends, indulge my Grief, and let me moum;
My *Cat* is gone, ah! never to return.
Now in my Study, all the tedious Night,
Alone I sit, and, unassisted, write:
Look often round (oh greatest Cause of Pain!)
And view the num'rous Labours of my Brain;
Those Quires of Words array'd in pompous Rhyme,
Which brav'd the Jaws of all-devouring Time;
Now undefended, and unwatch'd by *Cats*,
Are now doom'd Victims to the Teeth of *Rats*.

James Thomson

LISY'S PARTING WITH HER CAT

The dreadful hour with leaden pace approached,
Lashed fiercely on by unrelenting fate,
When Lisy and her bosom Cat must part:
For now, to school and pensive needle doomed,
She's banished from her childhood's undashed joy,
And all the pleasing intercourse she kept
With her grey comrade, which has often soothed
Her tender moments while the world around
Glowed with ambition, business, and vice,
Or lay dissolved in sleep's delicious arms;
And from their dewy orbs the conscious stars
Shed on their friendship influence benign.
　　But see where mournful Puss, advancing, stood
With outstretched tail, casts looks of anxious woe
On melting Lisy, in whose eyes the tear
Stood tremulous, and thus would fain have said,
If Nature had not tied her struggling tongue:
'Unkind, O! who shall now with fattening milk,
With flesh, with bread, and fish beloved, and meat,
Regale my taste? and at the cheerful fire,
Ah, who shall bask me in their downy lap?
Who shall invite me to the bed, and throw
The bedclothes o'er me in the winter night,
When Eurus roars? Beneath whose soothing hand
Soft shall I purr? But now, when Lisy's gone,
What is the dull officious world to me?
I loathe the thoughts of life:' Thus plained the cat,
While Lisy felt, by sympathetic touch,
These anxious thoughts that in her mind revolved,
And casting on her a desponding look,
She snatched her in her arms with eager grief,

And mewing, thus began: 'O Cat beloved!
Thou dear companion of my tender years!
Joy of my youth! that oft has licked my hands
With velvet tongue ne'er stained by mouse's blood.
Oh, gentle Cat! how shall I part with thee?
How dead and heavy will the moments pass
When you are not in my delighted eye,
With Cubi playing, or your flying tail.
How harshly will the softest muslin feel,
And all the silk of schools, while I no more
Have your sleek skin to soothe my softened sense?
How shall I eat while you are not beside
To share the bit? How shall I ever sleep
While I no more your lulling murmurs hear?
Yet we must part—so rigid fate decrees—
But never shall your loved idea dear
Part from my soul, and when I first can mark
The embroidered figure on the snowy lawn,
Your image shall my needle keen employ.
Hark! now I'm called away! O direful sound!
I come—I come, but first I charge you all—

You—you—and you, particularly you,
O, Mary, Mary, feed her with the best,
Repose her nightly in the warmest couch,
And be a Lisy to her!'—Having said,
She set her down, and with her head across,
Rushed to the evil which she could not shun,
While a sad mew went knelling to her heart!

Thomas Gray

ON THE DEATH OF A FAVOURITE CAT, DROWNED IN A TUB OF GOLD FISHES

'Twas on a lofty vase's side,
Where China's gayest art had dy'd
    The azure flowers that blow;
Demurest of the tabby kind,
The pensive Selima, reclin'd,
    Gaz'd on the lake below.

Her conscious tail her joy declar'd;
The fair round face, the snowy beard,
    The velvet of her paws,
Her coat, that with the tortoise vies,
Her ears of jet, and emerald eyes,
    She saw; and purr'd applause.

Still had she gaz'd; but 'midst the tide
Two angel forms were seen to glide,
    The Genii of the stream:
Their scaly armour's Tyrian hue
Thro' richest purple to the view
    Betray'd a golden gleam.

The hapless Nymph with wonder saw:
A whisker first, and then a claw,
    With many an ardent wish,
She stretch'd in vain to reach the prize.
What female heart can gold despise?
    What Cat's averse to fish?

Presumptuous Maid! with looks intent
Again she stretch'd, again she bent,
    Nor knew the gulf between.
(Malignant Fate sat by, and smil'd.)
The slipp'ry verge her feet beguil'd,
    She tumbled headlong in.

Eight times emerging from the flood
She mew'd to ev'ry wat'ry God,
    Some speedy aid to send,
No Dolphin came, no Nereid stirr'd:
Nor cruel Tom, nor Susan heard.
    A Fav'rite has no friend!

From hence, ye Beauties, undeceiv'd,
Know, one false step is ne'er retriev'd,
    And be with caution bold.
Not all that tempts your wand'ring eyes
And heedless hearts, is lawful prize;
    Nor all that glisters, gold.

Christopher Smart

from 'REJOICE IN THE LAMB' ('JUBILATE AGNO')

... For I will consider my Cat Jeoffry.

For he is the servant of the Living God, duly and daily serving him.

For at the first glance of the glory of God in the East he worships in his way.

For is this done by wreathing his body seven times round with elegant quickness.

For then he leaps up to catch the musk, which is the blessing of God upon his prayer.

For he rolls upon prank to work it in.

For having done duty and received blessing he begins to consider himself.

For this he performs in ten degrees.

For first he looks upon his fore-paws to see if they are clean.

For secondly he kicks up behind to clear away there.

For thirdly he works it upon stretch with the fore paws extended.

For fourthly he sharpens his paws by wood.

For fifthly he washes himself.

For Sixthly he rolls upon wash.

For Seventhly he fleas himself, that he may not be interrupted upon the beat.

For Eighthly he rubs himself against a post.

For Ninthly he looks up for his instructions.

For Tenthly he goes in quest of food.

For having considered God and himself he will consider his neighbour.

For if he meets another cat he will kiss her in kindness.

For when he takes his prey he plays with it to give it chance.

For one mouse in seven escapes by his dallying.

For when his day's work is done his business more properly begins.

For he keeps the Lord's watch in the night against the adversary.

For he counteracts the powers of darkness by his electrical skin and glaring eyes.

For he counteracts the Devil, who is death, by brisking about the life.

For in his morning orisons he loves the sun and the sun loves him.

For he is of the tribe of Tiger.

For the Cherub Cat is a term of the Angel Tiger.

For he has the subtlety and hissing of a serpent, which in goodness he suppresses.

For he will not do destruction, if he is well-fed, neither will he spit without provocation.

For he purrs in thankfulness, when God tells him he's a good Cat.

For he is an instrument for the children to learn benevolence upon.

For every house is incompleat without him and a blessing is lacking in the spirit.

For the Lord commanded Moses concerning the cats at the departure of the Children of Israel from Egypt.

For every family had one cat at least in the bag.

For the English Cats are the best in Europe.

For he is the cleanest in the use of his fore-paws of any quadrupede.

For the dexterity of his defence is an instance of the love of God to him exceedingly.

For he is the quickest to his mark of any creature.

For he is tenacious of his point.

For he is a mixture of gravity and waggery.

For he knows that God is his Saviour.

For there is nothing sweeter than his peace when at rest.

For there is nothing brisker than his life when in motion.

For he is of the Lord's poor and so indeed is he called by benevolence perpetually—Poor Jeoffry! poor Jeoffry! the rat has bit thy throat.

For I bless the name of the Lord Jesus that Jeoffry is better.

For the divine spirit comes about his body to sustain it in compleat cat.

For his tongue is exceeding pure so that it has in purity what it wants in musick.

For he is docile and can learn certain things.

For he can set up with gravity which is patience upon approbation.

For he can fetch and carry, which is patience in employment.

For he can jump over a stick which is patience upon proof positive.

For he can spraggle upon waggle at the word of command.

For he can jump from an eminence into his master's bosom.

For he can catch the cork and toss it again.

For he is hated by the hypocrite and miser.

For the former is affraid of detection.

For the latter refuses the charge.

For he camels his back to bear the first notion of business.

For he is good to think on, if a man would express himself neatly.

For he made a great figure in Egypt for his signal services.

For he killed the Ichneumon-rat very pernicious by land.

For his ears are so acute that they sting again.

For from this proceeds the passing quickness of his attention.

For by stroaking of him I have found out electricity.

For I perceived God's light about him both wax and fire.

For the Electrical fire is the spiritual substance, which God sends from heaven to sustain the bodies both of man and beast.

For God has blessed him in the variety of his movements.

For, tho he cannot fly, he is an excellent clamberer.

For his motions upon the face of the earth are more than any other quadrupede.

For he can tread to all the measures upon the musick.

For he can swim for life.

For he can creep.

William Cowper

THE COLUBRIAD

Close by the threshold of a door nail'd fast
Three kittens sat: each kitten look'd aghast.
I, passing swift and inattentive by,
At the three kittens cast a careless eye;
Not much concern'd to know what they did there,
Not deeming kittens worth a poet's care.
But presently a loud and furious hiss
Caused me to stop, and to exclaim—what's this?
When, lo! upon the threshold met my view,
With head erect, and eyes of fiery hue,
A viper, long as Count de Grasse's queue.
Forth from his head his forkèd tongue he throws,
Darting it full against a kitten's nose;
Who having never seen in field or house
The like, sat still and silent, as a mouse:
Only, projecting with attention due
Her whisker'd face, she ask'd him—who are you?
On to the hall went I, with pace not slow,
But swift as lightning, for a long Dutch hoe;
With which well arm'd I hasten'd to the spot,
To find the viper. But I found him not,
And, turning up the leaves and shrubs around,
Found only, that he was not to be found.
But still the kittens, sitting as before
Sat watching close the bottom of the door.
I hope—said I—the villain I would kill
Has slipt between the door and the door's sill;
And if I make dispatch, and follow hard,
No doubt but I shall find him in the yard—
For long ere now it should have been rehears'd,
'Twas in the garden that I found him first.

E'en there I found him; there the full-grown cat
His head with velvet paw did gently pat,
As curious as the kittens erst had been
To learn what this phenomenon might mean.
Fill'd with heroic ardour at the sight,
And fearing every moment he might bite,
And rob our household of our only cat
That was of age to combat with a rat,
With outstretched hoe I slew him at the door,
And taught him NEVER TO COME THERE NO MORE.

Anna Seward

AN OLD CAT'S DYING SOLILOQUY

Years saw me still Acasto's mansion grace,
The gentlest, fondest of the tabby race;
Before him frisking through the garden glade,
Or at his feet in quiet slumber laid;
Praised for my glossy back of zebra streak,
And wreaths of jet encircling round my neck;
Soft paws that ne'er extend the clawing nail,
The snowy whisker and the sinuous tail;
Now feeble age each glazing eyeball dims,
And pain has stiffened these once supple limbs;
Fate of eight lives the forfeit gasp obtains,
And e'en the ninth creeps languid through my veins.

Much sure of good the future has in store,
When on my master's hearth I bask no more,
In those blest climes, where fishes oft forsake
The winding river and the glassy lake;
There, as our silent-footed race behold
The crimson spots and fins of lucid gold,
Venturing without the shielding waves to play,
They gasp on shelving banks, our easy prey:
While birds unwinged hop careless o'er the ground,
And the plump mouse incessant trots around,
Near wells of cream that mortals never skim,
Warm marum creeping round their shallow brim;
Where green valerian tufts, luxuriant spread,
Cleanse the sleek hide and form the fragrant bed.*

Yet, stern dispenser of the final blow,
Before thou lay'st an aged grimalkin low,
Bend to her last request a gracious ear,

*The affection of cats for marum and valerian is well known. They will beat the
stems down, mat them with their feet, and then roll upon them. [A. S.]

Some days, some few short days, to linger here;
So to the guardian of his tabby's weal
Shall softest purrs these tender truths reveal:
    'Ne'er shall thy now expiring puss forget
To thy kind care her long-enduring debt,
Nor shall the joys that painless realms decree
Efface the comforts once bestowed by thee;
To countless mice thy chicken-bones preferred,
Thy toast to golden fish and wingless bird;
O'er marum borders and valerian bed
Thy Selima shall bend her moping head,
Sigh that no more she climbs, with grateful glee,
Thy downy sofa and thy cradling knee;
Nay, e'en at founts of cream shall sullen swear,
Since thou, her more loved master, art not there.'

Joanna Baillie

from THE KITTEN

Whence hast thou then, thou witless puss,
The magic power to charm us thus?
Is it that in thy glaring eye
And rapid movements, we descry—
Whilst we at ease, secure from ill,
The chimney corner snugly fill—
A lion darting on his prey,
A tiger at his ruthless play?
Or, is it, that in thee we trace
With all thy varied wanton grace,
An emblem, view'd with kindred eye,
Of tricky, restless infancy?
Ah! many a lightly sportive child,
Who hath like thee our wits beguiled,
To dull and sober manhood grown,
With strange recoil our hearts disown.
Even so, poor kit! must thou endure,
When thou become'st a cat demure,
Full many a cuff and angry word,
Chid roughly from the tempting board,
And yet, for that thou hast, I ween,
So oft our favoured playmate been,
Soft be the change, which thou shalt prove,
When time hath spoiled thee of our love;
Still be thou deem'd, by housewife fat,
A comely, careful, mousing cat,
Whose dish is, for the public good,
Replenish'd oft with savoury food.
Nor, when thy span of life be past,
Be thou to pond or dunghill cast;
But gently borne on goodman's spade,

Beneath the decent sod be laid,
And children show, with glistening eyes,
The place where poor old Pussy lies.

Walter Savage Landor

TO HIS YOUNG SON CARLINO IN ITALY, FROM ENGLAND

Does Cincirillo follow thee about?
Inverting one swart foot suspensively,
And wagging his dread jaw, at every chirp
Of bird above him on the olive-branch?
Frighten him then away! 'twas he who slew
Our pigeons, our white pigeons, peacock-tailed,
That fear'd not you and me ... alas, nor him!
I flattened his striped sides along my knee,
And reasoned with him on his bloody mind,
Till he looked blandly, and half-closed his eyes
To ponder on my lecture in the shade.
I doubt his memory much, his heart a little,
And in some minor matters (may I say it?)
Could wish him rather sager. But from thee
God hold back wisdom yet for many years!
Whether in early season or in late
It always comes high priced.

John Keats

TO A CAT

Cat! who hast pass'd thy grand climacteric,
    How many mice and rats hast in thy days
    Destroy'd?—How many titbits stolen? Gaze
With those bright languid segments green, and prick
Those velvet ears—but prythee do not stick
    Thy latent talons in me—and upraise
    Thy gentle mew—and tell me all thy frays
Of fish and mice, and rats and tender chick.
Nay, look not down, nor lick thy dainty wrists—
    For all the wheezy asthma,—and for all
Thy tail's tip is nick'd off—and though the fists
    Of many a maid have given thee many a maul,
Still is that fur as soft as when the lists
    In youth thou enter'dst on glass bottled wall.

Heinrich Heine

Translated by Elizabeth Barrett Browning

MEIN KIND, WIR WAREN KINDER

My child, we were two children,
Small, merry by childhood's law;
We used to crawl to the hen-house
And hide ourselves in the straw.

We crowed like cocks, and whenever
The passers near us drew—
Cock-a-doodle! they thought
'Twas a real cock that crew.

The boxes about our courtyard
We carpeted to our mind,
And lived there both together—
Kept house in a noble kind.

The neighbour's old cat often
Came to pay us a visit;
We made her a bow and curtsey,
Each with a compliment in it.

After her health we asked,
Our care and regard to evince—
(We have made the very same speeches
To many an old cat since).

Frederick Pollock

LINES ON THE DEATH OF A COLLEGE CAT

The Junior Fellow's vows were said;
Among his co-mates and their Head
    His place was fairly set.
Of welcome from friends old and new
Full dues he had, and more than due;
    What could be lacking yet?

One said, 'The Senior Fellow's vote!'
The Senior Fellow, black of coat,
    Save where his front was white,
Arose and sniffed the stranger's shoes
With critic nose, as ancients use
    To judge mankind aright.

I—for 'twas I who tell the tale—
Conscious of fortune's trembling scale,
    Awaited the decree;
But Tom had judged: 'He loves our race,'
And, as to his ancestral place,
    He leapt upon my knee.

Thenceforth in common-room and hall
A *verus socius* known to all
    I came and went and sat,
Far from cross fate's or envy's reach;
For none a title could impeach
    Accepted by the cat.

While statutes changed, and freshmen came,
His gait, his wisdom were the same,
   His age no more than mellow;
Yet nothing mortal may defy
The march of *Anno Domini*,
   Not e'en the Senior Fellow.

Beneath our linden shade he lies;
Mere eld hath softly closed his eyes
   With late and honoured end.
He seems, while catless we confer,
To join with faint Elysian purr,
   A tutelary friend.

Charles Baudelaire
Translated by D.S. MacColl

CATS

The fervent lover and the sage austere
In their ripe season equally admire
The great soft cats, who, like their masters dear,
Are shivery folk and sit beside the fire.

Friends both of learning and of wantonness,
They hunt where silence and dread shadows are;
Erebus would have yoked them to his car
For funeral coursers had their pride been less.

They take, brooding, the noble attitudes
Of sphinxes stretched in deepest solitudes
That look to slumber in an endless dream:
Their loins are quick with kindlings magical,
And glints of gold, as in a sandy stream,
Vaguely bestar their eyeballs mystical.

Charles Baudelaire

Translated by George Dillon

CATS

No-one but indefatigable lovers and old
Chilly philosophers can understand the true
Charm of these animals serene and potent, who
Likewise are sedentary and suffer from the cold.

They are the friends of learning and of sexual bliss;
Silence they love, and darkness where temptation breeds.
Erebus would have made them his funereal steeds,
Save that their proud free nature would not stoop to this.

Like those great sphinxes lounging through eternity
In noble attitudes upon the desert sand,
They gaze incuriously at nothing, calm and wise.

Their fecund loins give forth electric flashes, and
Thousands of golden particles drift ceaselessly,
Like galaxies of stars, in their mysterious eyes.

Charles Baudelaire
Translated by Roy Campbell

THE CAT

Come, my fine cat, against my loving heart;
 Sheathe your sharp claws, and settle.
And let my eyes into your pupils dart
 Where agate sparks with metal.

Now while my fingertips caress at leisure
 Your head and wiry curves,
And that my hand's elated with the pleasure
 Of your electric nerves,

I think about my woman—how her glances
 Like yours, dear beast, deep-down
And cold, can cut and wound one as with lances;

 Then, too, she has that vagrant
And subtle air of danger that makes fragrant
 Her body, lithe and brown.

Emily Dickinson

CAT

She sights a Bird—she chuckles—
She flattens—then she crawls—
She runs without the look of feet—
Her eyes increase to Balls—

Her jaws stir—twitching—hungry—
Her Teeth can hardly stand—
She leaps, but Robin leaped the first—
Ah, Pussy, of the Sand.

The Hopes so juicy ripening—
You almost bathed your Tongue—
When Bliss disclosed a hundred Toes—
And fled with every one—

Christina Rossetti

ON THE DEATH OF A CAT, A FRIEND OF MINE AGED TEN YEARS AND A HALF

Who shall tell the lady's grief
When her cat was past relief?
Who shall number the hot tears
Shed o'er her, belov'd for years?
Who shall say the dark dismay
Which her dying caused that day?

Come, ye Muses, one and all,
Come obedient to my call;
Come and mourn with tuneful breath
Each one for a separate death;
And, while you in numbers sigh,
I will sing her elegy.

Of a noble race she came,
And Grimalkin was her name.
Young and old full many a mouse
Felt the prowess of her house;
Weak and strong full many a rat
Cowered beneath her crushing pat;
And the birds around the place
Shrank from her too-close embrace.
But one night, reft of her strength,
She lay down and died at length:
Lay a kitten by her side
In whose life the mother died.
Spare her life and lineage,
Guard her kitten's tender age,

And that kitten's name as wide
Shall be known as hers that died.
And whoever passes by
The poor grave where Puss doth lie,
Softly, softly let him tread,
Nor disturb her narrow bed.

C.S. Calverley

SAD MEMORIES

They tell me I am beautiful: they praise my silken hair,
My little feet that silently slip on from stair to stair:
They praise my pretty trustful face and innocent grey eye;
Fond hands caress me oftentimes, yet would that I might die!

Why was I born to be abhorred of man and bird and beast?
The bullfinch marks me stealing by, and straight his song hath
    ceased;
The shrewmouse eyes me shudderingly, then flees; and, worse
    than that,
The housedog he flees after me—why was I born a cat?

Men prize the heartless hound who quits dry-eyed his native
    land;
Who wags a mercenary tail and licks a tyrant hand.
The leal true cat they prize not, that if e'er compelled to roam
Still flies, when let out of the bag, precipitately home.

They call me cruel. Do I know if mouse or song-bird feels?
I only know they make me light and salutary meals:
And if, as 'tis my nature to, ere I devour I tease 'em,
Why should a low-bred gardener's boy pursue me with a
    besom?

Should china fall or chandeliers, or anything but stocks—
Nay stocks, when they're in flowerpots—the cat expects hard
    knocks:
Should ever anything be missed—milk, coals, umbrellas,
    brandy—
The cat's pitched into with a boot or anything that's handy . . .

'I remember, I remember,' how one night I 'fleeted by,'
And gained the blessed tiles and gazed into the cold clear sky.
'I remember, I remember,' how my little lovers came;
And there, beneath the crescent moon, play'd many a little
 game.

They fought—by good St Catherine, 'twas a fearsome sight
 to see
The coal-black crest, the glowering orbs, of one gigantic He.
Like bow by some tall bowman bent at Hastings or Poictiers,
His huge back curved, till none observed a vestige of his ears:

He stood, an ebon crescent, flouting that ivory moon;
Then raised the pibroch of his race, the Song without a Tune;
Gleam'd his white teeth, his mammoth tail waved darkly to
 and fro,
As with one complex yell he burst, all claws, upon the foe.

It thrills me now, that final miaow—that weird unearthly din:
Lone maidens heard it far away, and leapt out of their skin.
A potboy from his den o'erhead peep'd with a scared wan
 face;
Then sent a random brickbat down, which knocked me into
 space.

Nine days I fell, or thereabouts: and, had we not nine lives,
I wish I ne'er had seen again thy sausage-shop, St Ives!
Had I, as some cats have, nine tails, how gladly I would lick
The hand, and person generally, of him who heaved that
 brick!

For me they fill the milkbowl up, and cull the choice sardine;
But ah! I nevermore shall be the cat I once have been!
The memories of that fatal night they haunt me even now:
In dreams I see that rampant He, and tremble at that Miaow.

Thomas Hardy

LAST WORDS TO A DUMB FRIEND

Pet was never mourned as you
Purrer of the spotless hue,
Plumy tail, and wistful gaze
While you humoured our queer ways,
Or outshrilled your morning call
Up the stairs and through the hall—
Foot suspended in its fall—
While expectant, you would stand
Arched to meet the stroking hand; -
Till your way you choose to wend
Yonder, to your tragic end.

Never another pet for me!
Let your place all vacant be;
Better blankness day by day
Than companion torn away.
Better bid his memory fade,
Better blot each mark he made,
Selfishly escape distress
By contrived forgetfulness,
Than preserve his prints to make
Every morn and eve an ache.

From the chair whereon he sat
Sweep his fur, nor wince thereat;
Rake his little pathways out
Mid the bushes roundabout;
Smooth away his talons' mark
From the claw-worn pine-tree bark,
Where he climbed as dusk embrowned,
Waiting us who loitered round.

Strange it is this speechless thing,
Subject to our mastering,
Subject for his life and food
To our gift, and time, and mood;
Timid pensioner of us Powers,
His existence ruled by ours,
Should—by crossing at a breath
Into safe and shielded death,
By the merely taking hence
Of his insignificance—
Loom as largened to the sense,
Shape as part, above man's will,
Of the Imperturbable.

As a prisoner, flight debarred,
Exercising in a yard,
Still retain I, troubled, shaken,
Mean estate, by him forsaken;
And this home, which scarcely took
Impress from his little look,
By his faring to the Dim
Grows all eloquent of him.

Housemate, I can think you still
Bounding to the window-sill,
Over which I vaguely see
Your small mound beneath the tree,
Showing in the autumn shade
That you moulder where you played.

Paul Verlaine

Translated by Arthur Symons

CAT AND LADY

They were at play, she and her cat,
And it was marvellous to mark
The white paw and the white hand pat
Each other in the deepening dark.

The stealthy little lady hid
Under her mittens' silken sheath
Her deadly agate nails that thrid
The silk-like dagger points of death.

The cat purred primly and drew in
Her claws that were of steel filed thin:
The devil was in it all the same.

And in the boudoir, while a shout
Of laughter in the air rang out,
Four sparks of phosphor shone like flame.

D.S. MacColl

CONNOISSEURS

Under a tree I read a Latin book,
And there, in seeming slumber, lies my cat;
Each of us thinking, with our harmless look,
Of this and that.

Such singing—prettier than any words—
O singers you are sweet and well-to-do!
My cat, who has the finest taste in birds,
Thinks so too.

W.B. Yeats

THE CAT AND THE MOON

The cat went here and there
And the moon spun round like a top,
And the nearest kin of the moon
The creeping cat looked up.
Black Minnaloushe stared at the moon,
For wander and wail as he would
The pure cold light in the sky
Troubled his animal blood.
Minnaloushe runs in the grass,
Lifting his delicate feet.
Do you dance, Minnaloushe, do you dance?
When two close kindred meet
What better than call a dance.
Maybe the moon may learn,
Tired of that courtly fashion,
A new dance turn.
Minnaloushe creeps through the grass
From moonlit place to place,
The sacred moon overhead
Has taken a new phase.
Does Minnaloushe know that his pupils
Will pass from change to change,
And that from round to crescent,
From crescent to round they range?
Minnaloushe creeps through the grass
Alone, important and wise,
And lifts to the changing moon
His changing eyes.

W.H. Davies

A CAT'S EXAMPLE

For three whole days I and my cat
Have come up here, and patiently sat—
    We sit and wait on silent Time;
He for a mouse that scratched close by,
At a hole where he sets his eye—
    And I for some music and rhyme.

Is this the Poet's secret, that
He waits in patience, like this cat,
    To start a dream from under cover?
A cat's example, too, in love,
With Passion's every trick and move,
    Would burn up any human lover.

Paul Valéry
Translated by David Paul

WHITE CATS
(*To Albert Dugrip*)

In the clear gold of sunlight, stretching their backs,
—White as snow—see the voluptuous cats,
Closing eyes jealous of their inner glooms,
Slumbering in the tepid warmth of their illumined fur.

Their coats have the dazzle of dawn-bathed glaciers.
Inside them, their bodies, frail, sinewy, and slender,
Feel the shiverings of a girl inside her dress,
And their beauty refines itself in endless languors.

No question but their Soul of old has animated
The flesh of a philosopher, or a woman's body,
For since then their dazzling and inestimable whiteness

Holding the mingled splendour of a grand premiere,
Ennobles them to a rank of calm contempt,
Indifferent to everything but Light itself!

Walter de le Mare

DOUBLE DUTCH

That crafty cat, a buff-black Siamese,
Sniffing through wild wood, sagely, silently goes,
Prick ears, lank legs, alertly twitching nose,
And on her secret errand reads with ease
A language no man knows.

FIVE EYES

In Hans' old Mill his three black cats
Watch his bins for the thieving rats.
Whisker and claw, they crouch in the night,
Their five eyes smouldering green and bright:
Squeaks from the flour sacks, squeaks from where
The cold wind stirs on the empty stair,
Squeaking and scampering, everywhere.
Then down they pounce, now in, now out,
At whisking tail, and sniffing snout;
While lean old Hans he snores away
Till peep of light at break of day;
Then up he climbs to his creaking mill,
Out come his cats all grey with meal —
Jekkel, and Jessup, and one-eyed Jill.

Robert Service

LOST KITTEN

Two men I saw reel from a bar
And stumble down the street;
Coarse and uncouth as workmen are,
They walked with wobbly feet.
I watched them, thinking sadly as
I heard their hobnails clink,
The only joy a toiler has
Is to get drowned in drink.

A kitten cowered on a wall,
A skinny, starving stray;
It looked so pitifully small,
A fluff of silver grey.
One of the men came to a stand,
A kindly chap was he,
For with a huge and horny hand
He stroked it tenderly.

With wistful hope it gazed at him
And arched a spine of fur;
It licked his hand so grimy grim
And feebly tried to purr.
And then it climbed upon his chest,
And to his drunken glee,
Upon his shoulder came to rest,
Contented as could be.

The other fellow with a jeer
Made feint to dash it down,
But as it shrank with sudden fear
I saw the first one frown;

And then I heard him coarsely cry:
'Have care for what you do;
Just harm a hair of it and I
Will twist my knife in you.'

So there they stood like brutes at bay,
Their blood at fighting heat;
And snarling at each other they
Went weaving down the street,
Leaving the kitten all alone
Upon its stoney shelf ...
And as I haven't heart of stone
I took it home myself.

Don Marquis

THE TOM-CAT

At midnight in the alley
    A Tom-cat comes to wail,
And he chants the hate of a million years
    As he swings his snaky tail.

Malevolent, bony, brindled,
    Tiger and devil and bard,
His eyes are coals from the middle of Hell
    And his heart is black and hard.

He twists and crouches and capers
    And bares his curved sharp claws,
And he sings to the stars of the jungle nights,
    Ere cities were, or laws.

Beast from a world primeval,
    He and his leaping clan,
When the blotched red moon leers over the roofs
    Give voice to their scorn of man.

He will lie on a rug tomorrow
    And lick his silky fur,
And veil the brute in his yellow eyes
    And play he's tame, and purr.

But at midnight in the alley
    He will crouch again and wail,
And beat the time for his demon's song
    With a swing of his demon's tail.

Don Marquis

THE SONG OF MEHITABEL

this is the song of mehitabel
of mehitabel the alley cat
as i wrote you before boss
mehitabel is a believer
in the pythagorean
theory of the transmigration
of the souls and she claims
that formerly her spirit
was incarnated in the body
of cleopatra
that was a long time ago
and one must not be
surprised if mehitabel
has forgotten some of her
more regal manners

i have had my ups and downs
but wotthehell wotthehell
yesterday sceptres and crowns
fried oysters and velvet gowns
and today i herd with bums
but wotthehell wotthehell
i wake the world from sleep
as i caper and sing and leap
when i sing my wild free tune
wotthehell wotthehell
under the blear eyed moon
i am pelted with cast off shoon
but wotthehell wotthehell

do you think that i would change
my present freedom to range
for a castle or moated grange
wotthehell wotthehell
cage me and i d go frantic
my life is so romantic
capricious and corybantic
and i m toujours gai toujours gai

i know that i am bound
for a journey down the sound
in the midst of a refuse mound
but wotthehell wotthehell
oh i should worry and fret
death and i will coquette
there s a dance in the old dame yet
toujours gai toujours gai

i once was an innocent kit
wotthehell wotthehell
with a ribbon my neck to fit
and bells tied onto it
o wotthehell wotthehell
but a maltese cat came by
with a come hither look in his eye
and a song that soared to the sky
and wotthehell wotthehell
and i followed adown the street
the pad of his rhythmical feet
o permit me again to repeat
wotthehell wotthehell

my youth i shall never forget
but there s nothing i really regret
wotthehell wotthehell

there s a dance in the old dame yet
toujours gai toujours gai
the things that i had not ought to
i do because i ve gotto
wotthehell wotthehell
and i end with my favourite motto
toujours gai toujours gai

boss sometimes i think
that our friend mehitabel
is a trifle too gay

Don Marquis

THE OLD TROUPER

i ran onto mehitabel again
last evening
she is inhabiting
a decayed trunk
which lies in an alley
in greenwich village
in company with the most
villainous tom cat
i have ever seen
but there is nothing
wrong about the association
archy she told me
it is merely a plutonic
attachment
and the thing can be
believed for the tom
looks like one of pluto s demons
it is a theatre trunk
archy mehitabel told me
and tom is an old theatre cat
he has given his life
to the theatre he claims that richard
mansfield once
kicked him out of the way
and then cried because
he had done it and
petted him
and at another time
he says in a case
of emergency
he played a bloodhound

in a production of
uncle tom s cabin
the stage is not what it
used to be tom says
he puts his front paw
on his breast and says
they don t have it any more
they don t have it here
the old troupers are gone
there s nobody can troupe
any more
they are all amateurs nowadays
they haven t got it
here
there are only
five or six of us oldtime
troupers left
this generation does not know
what stage presence is
personality is what they lack
personality

where would they get
the training my old friends
got in the stock companies
i knew mr booth very well
says tom
and a law should be passed
preventing anybody else
from ever playing
in any play he ever
played in
there was a trouper for you
i used to sit on his knee
and purr when i was

a kitten he used to tell me
how much he valued my opinion
finish is what they lack
finish
and they haven t got it
here
and again he laid his paw
on his breast
i remember mr daly very
well too
i was with mr daly s company
for several years
there was art for you
there was team work
there was direction
they knew the theatre
and they all had it
here
for two years mr daly
would not ring up the curtain
unless i was in the
prompter s box
they are amateurs nowadays
rank amateurs all of them
for two seasons i played
the dog in joseph
jefferson s rip van winkle
it is true i never came
on the stage
but he knew i was just off
and it helped him
i would like to see
one of your modern
theatre cats
act a dog so well

that it would convince
a trouper like jo jefferson
but they haven t got it
nowadays
they haven t got it
here
jo jefferson had it he had it
here

i come of a long line
of theatre cats
my grandfather
was with forrest
he had it he was a real trouper
my grandfather said
he had a voice
that used to shake
the ferryboats
on the north river
once he lost his beard
and my grandfather
dropped from the
fly gallery and landed
under his chin
and played his beard
for the rest of the act
you don t see any theatre
cats that could do that
nowadays
they haven t got it they
haven t got it
here
once i played the owl
in modjeska s production
of macbeth

i sat above the castle gate
in the murder scene
and made my yellow
eyes shine through the dusk
like an owl s eyes
modjeska was a real
trouper she knew how to pick
her support i would like
to see any of these modern
theatre cats play the owl s eyes
to modjeska s lady macbeth
but they haven t got it nowadays
they haven t got it
here

mehitabel he says
both our professions
are being ruined
by amateurs
                              archy

Edward Thomas

A CAT

She had a name among the children;
But no one loved though some one owned
Her, locked her out of doors at bedtime,
And had her kittens duly drowned.

In spring, nevertheless, this cat
Ate blackbirds, thrushes, nightingales,
And birds of bright voice, and plume, and flight,
As well as scraps from neighbours' pails.

I loathed and hated her for this;
One speckle on a thrush's breast
Was worth a million such; and yet
She lived long, till God gave her rest.

Harold Monro

MILK FOR THE CAT

When the tea is brought at five o'clock,
And all the neat curtains are drawn with care,
The little black cat with bright green eyes
Is suddenly purring there.

At first she pretends, having nothing to do,
She has come in merely to blink by the grate,
But though tea may be late or the milk may be sour,
She is never late.

And presently her agate eyes
Take a soft large milky haze,
And her independent casual glance
Becomes a stiff, hard gaze.

Then she stamps her claws or lifts her ears
Or twists her tail and begins to stir,
Till suddenly all her lithe body becomes
One breathing, trembling purr.

The children eat and wriggle and laugh;
The two old ladies stroke their silk:
But the cat is grown small and thin with desire,
Transformed to a creeping lust for milk.

The white saucer like some full moon descends
At last from the cloud of the table above;
She sighs and dreams and thrills and glows,
Transfigured with love.

She nestles over the shining rim,
Buries her chin in the creamy sea;
Her tail hangs loose; each drowsy paw
Is doubled under each bending knee.

A long dim ecstasy holds her life;
Her world is an infinite shapeless white,
Till her tongue has curled the last holy drop
Then she sinks back into the night,

Draws and dips her body to heap
Her sleepy nerves in the great arm-chair,
Lies defeated and buried deep
Three or four hours unconscious there.

Lytton Strachey

THE CAT

Dear creature by the fire a-purr,
    Strange idol eminently bland,
Miraculous puss! As o'er your fur
    I trail a negligible hand,

And gaze into your gazing eyes,
    And wonder in a demi-dream
What mystery it is that lies
    Behind those slits that glare and gleam,

An exquisite enchantment falls
    About the portals of my sense;
Meandering through enormous halls
    I breathe luxurious frankincense,

An ampler air, a warmer June
    Enfold me, and my wondering eye
Salutes a more imperial moon
    Throned in a more resplendent sky

Than ever knew this northern shore.
    O, strange! For you are with me too,
And I who am a cat once more
    Follow the woman that was you.

With tail erect and pompous march,
    The proudest puss that ever trod,
Through many a grove, 'neath many an arch,
    Impenetrable as a god,

Down many an alabaster flight
    Of broad and cedar-shaded stairs,
While over us the elaborate night
    Mysteriously gleams and glares!

Guillaume Apollinaire

JE SOUHAITE DANS MA MAISON

Je souhaite dans ma maison:
une femme ayant sa raison,
un chat passant parmi les livres,
des amis en toute saison
sans lesquels je ne peux pas vivre.

In my house I wish to find:
a woman of sound mind,
amongst the books a cat,
and friends at all times.
I cannot live without that.

Translated by Bridget Farrell

Alexander Gray

ON A CAT AGING

He blinks upon the hearth-rug
And yawns in deep content,
Accepting all the comforts
That Providence has sent.

Louder he purrs, and louder,
In one glad hymn of praise,
For all the night's adventures,
For quiet, restful days.

Life will go on for ever,
With all that cat can wish;
Warmth, and the glad procession
Of fish, and milk and fish.

Only—the thought disturbs him—
He's noticed once or twice,
The times are somehow breeding
A nimbler race of mice.

Frances Cornford

ON MAOU DYING AT THE AGE OF SIX MONTHS

Strange sickness fell upon this perfect creature
Who walked the equal friend of Man and Nature.
Her little Bodie, e'en as by a shroud,
Lay lapped in its unseen, dishevelling cloud;
Till to her eyes, unasking but afraid,
The old reply of endless night was made.

T.S. Eliot

from THE LOVE SONG OF J. ALFRED PRUFROCK

The yellow fog that rubs its back upon the window-panes,
The yellow smoke that rubs its muzzle on the window-panes
Licked its tongue into the corners of the evening,
Lingered upon the pools that stand in drains,
Let fall upon its back the soot that falls from chimneys,
Slipped by the terrace, made a sudden leap,
And seeing that it was a soft October night,
Curled once about the house, and fell asleep.

Howard Phillips Lovecraft

ON THE DEATH OF A MUCH-LOVED
KITTEN NAMED SAM PERKINS

The ancient garden seems at night
A deeper gloom to bear,
As if some silent shadow's blight
Were hov'ring in the air.

With hidden griefs the grasses sway,
Unable quite to word them—
Remembering from yesterday
The little paws that stirred them.

'Michael Scot' (Kathleen Goodfellow)

BALLADE OF THE CATS OF BYGONE TIME

Where is the Cat with the Fiddle gone?
The Cats of Kilkenny? The Cheshire? Ah!
Where is the Cat of Dick Whittington?
And Puss-in-Boots, Marquis of Carabas?
In Paradise, or in Nirvana?
Louis Wain's Cats in their ties and spats?
In Lost Atlantis? In Valhalla?
Tell me where is the King of the Cats?

Black, white, yellow, grey, striped, or brown:
Felix the Cat of the Cinema,
The Cat that went up to London Town,
The Cats of Baudelaire (Oh! la! la!),
Fanchette (also from Lutetia),
Where are they hunting for shining rats?
Through what wild nights of Arabia?
Tell me where is the King of the Cats?

Moon-bright Minnaloushe, Pangur Bán,
Tobermory who talked (Aha!),
Tiger-lily, Topaz (my own),
The Cat Hodge (felis Johnsonia):
Crunch they what fishy ambrosia?
Lap they what nectar from creaming vats?
In Tir-n'an-Og? In Arcadia?
Tell me where is the King of the Cats?

Siamese King and Persian Shah!
Cry from your Courts (or your service flats)
Où (dites-moi)—sont tous ces chats?
Tell me where is the King of the Cats?

Victoria Sackville-West

THE GREATER CATS

The greater cats with golden eyes
Stare out between the bars.
Deserts are there, and different skies,
And night with different stars.
They prowl the aromatic hill,
And mate as fiercely as they kill,
And hold the freedom of their will
To roam, to live, to drink their fill;
But this beyond their wit know I:
Man loves a little, and for long shall die.

Their kind across the desert range
Where tulips spring from stones,
Not knowing they will suffer change
Or vultures pick their bones.
Their strength's eternal in their sight,
They rule the terror of the night,
They overtake the deer in flight,
And in their arrogance they smite;
But I am sage, if they are strong:
Man's love is transient as his death is long.

Yet oh, what powers to deceive!
My wit is turned to faith,
And at this moment I believe
In love, and scout at death.
I came from nowhere, and shall be
Strong, steadfast, swift, eternally:
I am a lion, a stone, a tree,
And as the Polar star in me
Is fixed my constant heart on thee.
Ah, may I stay for ever blind
With lions, tigers, leopards, and their kind.

Dorothy L. Sayers

WAR CAT

I am sorry, my little cat, I am sorry—
If I had it, you should have it;
But there is a war on.

No, there are no table-scraps;
there was only an omelette
made from dehydrated eggs,
and baked apples to follow,
and we finished it all.
The butcher has no lights,
the fishmonger has no cod's heads—
there is nothing for you
but cat-biscuit
and those remnants of yesterday's ham;
you must do your best with it.

Round and pathetic eyes,
baby mouth opened in a reproachful cry,
how can I explain to you ?
I know, I know:
'Mistress, it is not nice;
the ham is very salt
and the cat-biscuit very dull,
I sniffed at it, and the smell was not enticing.
Do you not love me any more?
Mistress, I do my best for the war-effort;
I killed four mice last week,
yesterday I caught a young stoat,
you stroked and praised me,
you called me a clever cat,
What have I done to offend you?

I am industrious, I earn my keep;
I am not like the parrot, who sits there
using bad language and devouring
parrot-seed at eight-and-sixpence a pound
without working for it.
If you will not pay me my wages
there is no justice;
If you have ceased to love me
there is no charity.

'See, now, I rub myself against your legs
to express my devotion,
which is not altered by any unkindness.
My little heart is contracted
because your goodwill is withdrawn from me;
my ribs are rubbing together
for lack of food,
but indeed I cannot eat this—
my soul revolts at the sight of it.
I have tried, believe me,
but it was like ashes in my mouth.
If your favour is departed
and your bowels of compassion are shut up,
then all that is left me
is to sit in a draught on the stone floor and look miserable
till I die of starvation
and a broken heart.'

Cat with the innocent face,
What can I say?
Everything is very hard on everybody.
If you were a little Greek cat,
or a little Polish cat,
there would be nothing for you at all,
not even cat-food:

indeed, you would be lucky
if you were not eaten yourself.
Think if you were a little Russian cat
prowling among the cinders of a deserted city!
Consider that pains and labour
and the valour of merchant-seamen and fishermen
have gone even to the making of this biscuit
which smells so unappetising.
Alas! there is no language
in which I can tell you these things.

Well, well!
if you will not be comforted
we will put the contents of your saucer
into the chicken-bowl—there!
all gone! nasty old cat-food—
The hens, I dare say,
will be grateful for it.

Wait only a little
and I will go to the butcher
and see if by any chance
he can produce some fragments of the insides of something.

Only stop crying
and staring in that unbearable manner—
as soon as I have put on my hat
we will try to do something about it.

My hat is on,
I have put on my shoes,
I have taken my shopping basket—
What are you doing on the table?

The chicken-bowl is licked clean;

there is nothing left in it at all.
Cat,
hell-cat, Hitler-cat, human,
all-too-human cat,
cat corrupt, infected,
instinct with original sin,
cat of a fallen and perverse creation,
hypocrite with the innocent and limpid eyes—
is nothing desirable
till somebody else desires it?

Is anything and everything attractive
so long as it is got by stealing?
Furtive and squalid cat,
green glance, squinted over a cringing shoulder,
streaking hurriedly out of the back door
in expectation of judgment,
your manners and morals are perfectly abhorrent to me,
you dirty little thief and liar.

Nevertheless,
although you have made a fool of me,
yet, bearing in mind your pretty wheedling ways
(not to mention the four mice and the immature stoat),
and having put on my hat to go to the butcher's,
I may as well go.

Robert Graves

CAT-GODDESSES

A perverse habit of cat-goddesses—
Even the best of them, black as coals
Save for a new moon blazing on each breast,
With coral tongues and beryl eyes like lamps,
Long-legged, pacing three by three in nines—
This obstinate habit is to yield themselves,
In verisimilar love-ecstasies,
To tatter-eared and slinking alley-toms,
No less below the common run of cats
Than they above it; which they do for spite,
To provoke jealousy—not the least abashed
By such gross-headed, rabbit-coloured litters
As soon they shall be happy to desert.

Ruth Pitter

QUORUM PORUM

In a dark Garden, by a dreadful Tree,
The Druid Toms were met. They numbered three:
Tab Tiger, Demon Black, and Ginger Hate.
Their forms were tense, their eyes were full of fate.
Save for the involuntary caudal thrill,
The horror was that they should sit so still.
An hour of ritual silence passed: then low
And marrow-freezing, Ginger moaned OROW,
Two horrid syllables of hellish lore,
Followed by deeper silence than before.
Another hour, the tabby's turn is come:
Rigid, he rapidly howls MUM MUM MUM,
Then reassumes his silence like a pall,
Clothed in negation, a dumb oracle.
At the third hour, the Black gasps out AH BLURK
Like a lost soul that founders in the mirk,
And the grim, ghastly, damned, and direful crew
Resumes its voiceless vigilance anew.
The fourth hour passes. Suddenly all three
Chant WEGGY WEGGY WEGGY mournfully,
Then stiffly rise, and melt into the shade,
Their Sabbath over, and their demons laid.

Geoffrey Taylor

CRUEL CLEVER CAT

Sally, having swallowed cheese,
Directs down holes the scented breeze,
Enticing thus with bated breath.
Nice mice to an untimely death.

E.V. Rieu

THE LOST CAT

She took a last and simple meal when there were none to see her
    steal—
    A jug of cream upon the shelf, a fish prepared for dinner;
And now she walks a distant street with delicately sandalled feet,
    And no one gives her much to eat or weeps to see her thinner.

O my beloved come again, come back in joy, come back in pain,
    To end our searching with a mew, or with a purr our grieving;
And you shall have for lunch or tea whatever fish swim in the sea
    And all the cream that's meant for me—and not a word of
        thieving!

Francis Stuart

SHE CANNOT READ

She cannot read
She cannot write
She cannot bark
She does not bite
My dear companion day and night

Nerissa Garnett
Aged 11 (daughter of David Garnett)

A SLEEPING SHAPE LIES ON THE BED

A sleeping shape lies on the bed
A cat morose, at peace, well-fed.
O Puss, you sleeping mass of fur,
Give me your voice and let me purr.

Stevie Smith

THE SINGING CAT

It was a little captive cat
    Upon a crowded train
His mistress takes him from his box
    To ease his fretful pain.

She holds him tight upon her knee
    The graceful animal
And all the people look at him
    He is so beautiful

But oh he pricks and oh he prods
    And turns upon her knee
Then lifteth up his innocent voice
    In plaintive melody.

He lifteth up his innocent voice
    He lifteth up, he singeth
And to each human countenance
    A smile of grace he bringeth.

He lifteth up his innocent paw
    Upon her breast he clingeth
And everybody cries, Behold
    The cat, the cat that singeth.

He lifteth up his innocent voice
    He lifteth up, he singeth
And all the people warm themselves
    In the love his beauty bringeth.

Stevie Smith

MONSIEUR PUSSY-CAT, BLACKMAILER

C'est un grand Monsieur Pussy-Cat
Who lives on the mat
Devant un feu énorme
And that is why he is so fat,
En effet il sait quelque chose
Et fait chanter son hôte,
Raison de plus pourquoi
He has such a glossy coat.
Ah ha, Monsieur Pussy-Cat,
Si grand et si gras,
Take care you don't *pousser trop*
The one who gives you such *jolis plats.*

Stevie Smith

MY CAT MAJOR

Major is a fine cat
What is he at?
He hunts birds in the hydrangea
And in the tree
Major was ever a ranger
He ranges where no one can see.

Sometimes he goes up to the attic
With a hooped back
His paws hit the iron rungs
Of the ladder in a quick kick
How can this be done?
It is a knack.

Oh Major is a fine cat
He walks cleverly
And what is he at, my fine cat?
No one can see.

Ewart Milne

DIAMOND CUT DIAMOND

Two cats
One up a tree
One under the tree
The cat up a tree is he
The cat under the tree is she
The tree is wych elm, just incidentally.
He takes no notice of she, she takes no notice of he.
He stares at the woolly clouds passing, she stares at the tree.
There's been a lot written about cats, by Old Possum, Yeats, and Company,
But not Alfred de Musset or Lord Tennyson or Poe or anybody
Wrote about one cat under, and one cat up, a tree.
God knows why this should be left to me
Except I like cats as cats be
Especially one cat up
And one cat under
A wych elm
Tree.

Cecil Day-Lewis

CAT

Tearaway kitten or staid mother of fifty,
Persian, Chinchilla, Siamese
Or backstreet brawler—you all have a tiger in your blood
And eyes opaque as the sacred mysteries.

The hunter's instinct sends you pouncing, dallying,
Formal and wild as a temple dance.
You take from man what is your due—the fireside saucer,
And give him his—a purr of tolerance.

Like poets you wrap your solitude around you
And catch your meaning unawares:
With consequential trot or frantic tarantella
You follow up your top-secret affairs.

Simpkin, our pretty cat, assumes my lap
As a princess her rightful throne,
Pads round and drops asleep there. Each is a familiar
Warmth to the other, each no less alone.

A.S.J. Tessimond

CATS

Cats no less liquid than their shadows
Offer no angles to the wind.
They slip, diminished, neat, through loopholes
Less than themselves; will not be pinned

To rules or routes for journeys; counter
Attack with non-resistance; twist
Enticing through the curving fingers
And leave an angered, empty fist.

They wait obsequious as darkness
Quick to retire, quick to return;
Admit no aim or ethics; flatter
With reservations; will not learn

To answer to their names; are seldom
Truly owned till shot or skinned.
Cats, no less liquid than their shadows
Offer no angles to the wind.

Louis MacNeice

THE DEATH OF A CAT

I

Since then, those months ago, these rooms miss something,
A link, a spark, and the street down there reproves
My negligence, particularly the gap
For the new block which, though the pile of timber
Is cleared on which he was laid to die, remains
A gap, a catch in the throat, a missing number.

You were away when I lost him, he had been absent
Six nights, two dead, which I had not learnt until
You returned and asked and found how he had come back
To a closed door having scoured the void of Athens
For who knows what and at length, more than unwell
Came back and less than himself, his life in tatters.

Since when I dislike that gap in the street and that obdurate
Dumb door of iron and glass and I resent
This bland blank room like a doctor's consulting room
With its too many exits, all of glass and frosted,
Through which he lurked and fizzed, a warm retort,
Found room for his bag of capers, his bubbling flasket.

For he was our puck, our miniature lar, he fluttered
Our dovecot of visiting cards, he flicked them askew,
The joker among them who made a full house. As you said,
He was a fine cat. Though how strange to have, as you said
    later,
Such a personal sense of loss. And looking aside
You said, but unconvincingly: What does it matter?

II

To begin with he was a beautiful object:
Blue crisp fur with a white collar,
Paws of white velvet, springs of steel,
A Pharaoh's profile, a Krishna's grace,
Tail like a questionmark at a masthead
And eyes dug out of a mine, not the dark
Clouded tarns of a dog's, but cat's eyes—
Light in a rock crystal, light distilled
Before his time and ours, before cats were tame.

To continue, he was alive and young,
A dancer, incurably male, a clown,
With his gags, his mudras, his entrechats,
His triple bends and his double takes,
Firm as a Rameses in African wonderstone,
Fluid as Krishna chasing the milkmaids,
Who hid under carpets and nibbled at olives,
Attacker of ankles, nonesuch of nonsense,
Indolent, impudent, cat catalytic.

To continue further: if not a person
More than a cipher, if not affectionate
More than indifferent, if not volitive
More than automaton, if not self-conscious
More than mere conscious, if not useful
More than a parasite, if allegorical
More than heraldic, if man-conditioned
More than a gadget, if perhaps a symbol
More than a symbol, if somewhat a proxy
More than a stand-in—was what he was!
A self-contained life, was what he must be
And is not now: more than an object.

And is not now. Spreadeagled on coverlets—
Those are the coverlets, bouncing on chairbacks—
These are the chairs, pirouetting and sidestepping,
Feinting and jabbing, breaking a picture frame—
Here is the picture, tartar and sybarite,
One minute quicksilver, next minute butterballs,
Precise as a fencer, lax as an odalisque,
And in his eyes the light from the mines
One minute flickering, steady the next,
Lulled to a glow or blown to a blaze,
But always the light that was locked in the stone
Before his time and ours; at best semi-precious
All stones of that kind yet, if not precious,
Are more than stones, beautiful objects
But more than objects. While there is light in them.

III

Canyons of angry sound, catastrophe, cataclysm,
Smells and sounds in cataracts, cat-Athens,
Not, not the Athens we know, each whisker buzzing
Like a whole Radar station, typhoons of grapeshot,
Crossfire from every roof of ultra-violet arrows
And in every gutter landmines, infra-red,
A massed barrage of too many things unknown
On too many too quick senses (cossetted senses
Of one as spoilt as Pangur Ban, Old Foss
Or My Cat Jeoffrey), all the drab and daily
Things to him deadly, all the blunt things sharp,
The paving stones a sword dance. Chanting hawkers
Whose street cries consecrate their loaves and fishes
And huge black chessmen carved out of old priests
And steatopygous boys, they all were Gogs and Magogs
With seven-league battering boots and hair-on-ending voices

Through which he had to dodge. And all the wheels
Of all the jeeps, trucks, trams, motor-bicycles, buses, sports
    cars,
Caught in his brain and ravelled out his being
To one high horrible twang of breaking catgut,
A swastika of lightning. Such was Athens
To this one indoors cat, searching for what
He could not grasp through what he could not bear,
Dragged to and fro by unseen breakers, broken
At last by something sudden; then dragged back

By his own obstinate instinct, a long dark thread
Like Ariadne's ball of wool in the labyrinth
Not now what he had played with as a kitten
But spun from his own catsoul, which he followed
Now that the minotaur of machines and men
Had gored him, followed it slowly, slowly, until
It snapped a few yards short of a closed door,
Of home, and he lay on his side like a fish on the pavement
While the ball of wool rolled back and down the hill,
His purpose gone, only his pain remaining
Which, even if purpose is too human a word,
Was not too human a pain for a dying cat.

IV

Out of proportion? Why, almost certainly.
You and I, darling, knew no better
Than to feel worse for it. As one feels worse
When a tree is cut down, an ear-ring lost,
A week-end ended, a child at nurse
Weaned. Which are also out of proportion.

Sentimentality? Yes, it is possible;
You and I, darling, are not above knowing

The tears of the semi-, less precious things,
A pathetic fallacy perhaps, as the man
Who gave his marble victory wings
Was the dupe—who knows—of sentimentality.

Not really classic. The Greek Anthology
Laments its pets (like you and me, darling),
Even its grasshoppers; dead dogs bark
On the roads of Hades where poets hung
Their tiny lanterns to ease the dark.
Those poets were late though. Not really classical.

Yet more than an object? Why, most certainly.
You and I, darling, know that sonatas
Are more than sound and that green grass
Is more than grass or green, which is why
Each of our moments as they pass
Is of some moment; more than an object.

So this is an epitaph, not for calamitous
Loss but for loss; this was a person
In a small way who had touched our lives
With a whisk of delight, like a snatch of a tune
From which one whole day's mood derives.
For you and me, darling, this is an epitaph.

Norman MacCaig

BLACK CAT IN A MORNING

Black cat, slink longer: flatten through the grass.
The chaffinch scolds you, pebbling you with chinks
Of quartzy sound, where the green lilac banks
White falls of stillness and green shades of peace.

A shape where topaz eyes may climb and find
The fluttering gone, the dust smelling of green,
The green a royal deshabille of the sun
Tossed on a tree and stitched with its own gold.

And chaffinch rattling from another bush
Shakes with his furious ounce a yard of leaves,
Strikes flints together in his soft throat and moves
In out, out in, two white stripes and a blush.

Black cat pours to the ground, is pool, is cat
That walks finicking away, twitching behind
A stretched foot: sits, is carved, upon the ground,
Drubbing soft tomtoms in his silky throat.

He changes all around him to his scale.
Suburban suns are jungle stripes of fire
And all the mornings that there ever were
Make this one mount and mount and overspill.

And in their drenching where time cannot be,
Amiably blinking in ancestral suns
He swallows chaffinches in stretching yawns
And holds the world down under one soft paw.

Francis Scarfe

OLD CATS

Those who love cats which do not even purr,
Or which are thin and tired and very old,
Bend down to them in the street and stroke their fur
And rub their ears and smooth their breast, and hold
Their paws, and gaze into their eyes of gold.

Hal Summers

MY OLD CAT

My old cat is dead,
Who would butt me with his head.
He had the sleekest fur.
He had the blackest purr.
Always gentle with us
Was this black puss,
But when I found him today
Stiff and cold where he lay
His look was a lion's
Full of rage, defiance:
Oh, he would not pretend
That what came was a friend
But met it in pure hate.
Well died, my old cat.

Roy Fuller

THE FAMILY CAT

This cat was bought upon the day
That marked the Japanese defeat;
He was anonymous and gay,
But timorous and not discreet.

Although three years have gone, he shows
Fresh sides of his uneven mind:
To us—fond, lenient—he grows
Still more eccentric and refined.

He is a grey, white-chested cat,
And barred with black along the grey;
Not large, and the reverse of fat,
His profile good from either way.

The poet buys especial fish,
Which is made ready by his wife;
The poet's son holds out the dish:
They thus maintain the creature's life.

It's not his anniversary
Alone that's his significance:
In any case mortality
May not be thought of in his presence.

For brief as are our lives, more brief
Exist. Our stroking hides the bones,
Which none the less cry out in grief
Beneath the mocking, loving tones.

Roy Fuller

IN MEMORY OF MY CAT DOMINO: 1951–1966

Rising at dawn to pee, I thought I saw you
Curved in a chair, with head raised to look at me,
As you did at such hours. But the next moment,
More used to the gloom, there was only a jar
And a face-cloth. Time enough, nonetheless,
For love's responsibilities to return
To me.
              The unique character of the dead
Is the source of our sense of mourning and loss;
So, back in bed, I avoided calling up
What I know is intact in my mind, your life,
Entirely possessed as it was by my care.

I could conceive you not as dead but merely
Gone before me to a world that sends to us
Decreasing intimations of its beings—
No doubt because they find us in the end
Pathetic, worthy, but of small importance.

So long had we been together it never
Occurred to me I might fall somewhat behind.
Even when, familiar fur in my hands,
The sickly wave of barbiturate rose up,
I thought it was I who was journeying on—
But looking back there is only emptiness,
Your dusty medicaments and my portrait
Taken with you: sad mode of life you've outpaced.

Douglas Stewart

from LADY FEEDING THE CATS

Shuffling along in her broken shoes from the slums,
A blue-eyed lady showing the weather's stain,
Her long dress green and black like a pine in the rain,
Her bonnet much bedraggled, daily she comes
Uphill past the Moreton Bays and the smoky gums
With a sack of bones on her back and a song in her brain
To feed those outlaws prowling about the Domain,
Those furtive she-cats and those villainous toms.

Proudly they step to meet her, they march together
With an arching of backs and a waving of plumy tails
And smiles; they swear they never would harm a feather.
They rub at her legs for the bounty that never fails,
 They think she is a princess out of a tower,
 And so she is, she is trembling with love and power.

Gavin Ewart

SONNET: CAT LOGIC

Cat sentimentality is a human thing. Cats
are indifferent, their minds can't comprehend
the concept 'I shall die', they just go on living.
Death is more foreign to their thought than
to us the idea of a lime-green lobster. That's
why holding these warm containers of purring fur
is poignant, that they just don't *know*.
Life is in them, like the brandy in the bottle.

One morning a cat wakes up, and doesn't feel
disposed to eat or wash or walk. It doesn't panic
or scream: 'My last hour has come!' It
simply fades. Cats never go grey at the edges
like us, they don't even look old. Peter Pans,
insouciant. No wonder people identify with cats.

A 14-YEAR OLD CONVALESCENT CAT IN THE WINTER

I want him to have another living summer,
to lie in the sun and enjoy the *douceur de vivre*—
because the sun, like golden rum in a rummer,
is what makes an idle cat *un tout petit peu ivre*—

I want him to lie stretched out, contented,
revelling in the heat, his fur all dry and warm,
an Old Age Pensioner, retired, resented
by no one, and happinesses in a beelike swarm

to settle on him—postponed for another season
that last fated hateful journey to the vet
from which there is no return (and age the reason),
which must soon come—as I cannot forget.

Gavin Ewart

'JUBILATE MATTEO'

For I rejoice in my cat Matty.

For his coat is variegated in black and brown, with white undersides.

For in every way his whiskers are marvellous.

For he resists the Devil and is completely neuter.

For he sleeps and washes himself and walks warily in the ways of Putney.

For he is at home in the whole district of SW 15.

For in this district the great Yorkshire Murderer ate his last meal before he entered into captivity.

For in the Book of Crime there is no name like John Reginald Halliday Christie.

For Yorkshire indeed excels in all things, as Geoffrey Boycott is the best Batsman.

For the Yorkshire Ripper and the Hull Arsonist have their horns exalted in glory.

For Yorkshire is therefore acknowledged the greatest County.

For Hull was once of the company, that is now of Humberside.

For Sir Leonard Hutton once scored 364 runs in a Test Match.

For Fred Trueman too is a flagrant glory to Yorkshire.

For my cat wanders in the ways of the angels of Yorkshire.

For in his soul God has shown him a remarkable vision of Putney.

For he has also trodden in the paths of the newly fashionable.

For those who live in Gwendolen Avenue cry 'Drop dead, darling!'

For in Cambalt Road and Dealtry Road where the Vet lives there are professional people.

For Erpingham Road and Danemere Street and Dryburgh Road include the intelligentsia.

For in Clarendon Drive the British Broadcasting Corporation is rampant.

For the glory of God has deserted the simple.

For the old who gossiped in Bangalore Road are unknown to the dayspring.

For there is a shortage of the old people who adorned the novels of William Trevor.

For in the knowledge of this I cling to the old folk ways of Gwalior Road and Olivette Street.

For I rejoice in my cat, who has the true spirit of Putney.

Charles Causley

IN SAN REMO

Deep in the garden of the Villa Tennyson,
Under a fig tree, end of the orange walk
(Where, in his life, he'd often sprawl and snooze)
Lies the good gatto Foss, for sixteen years
Daily companion of Edward Lear.

Subject of scurrilous drawings, calumnies,
Foss soldiered on, ignoring jokes about
His half-of-tail, his gig-lamp eyes, his noisy
Stripes, the slur that having grown so fat
He couldn't navigate an open door,

But Foss, the wise old Greek out of Corfu,
Took it all in his stride, as if he knew
This from the shyest, oddest Englishman
Was declaration of a profound love.
A white stone, neatly cut, inscribed in best

Italian tells Foss's history. No one
Was much surprised when in a month or two,
His owlish, foreign friend, bereft of company,
Had followed him. The English Cemetery
Next day was closed, as if for lunch, but glancing

Through the stern gates I saw a cat, two kittens
Processing gravely down the central avenue,
Never turning. Suddenly prancing. Dancing.

John Heath-Stubbs

'JEOFFREY'

For I will consider my master Christopher

For he also is the servant of the living God

For he yowls at all hours singing psalms

For he is of the house of Asaph the chief musician

For all poets are of the royal household of David

For deprived of ink and paper he scrawls verses on the door
    of his prison with a key

For he prays naked in the rain—but I do not accompany him
    in this

For I have too much concern for my fur which is the robe of
    honour the Lord has given me

For he has no passion for clean linen, and is lousy

For he could seek better instruction from me in these matters

For maybe he spares his lice out of charity

For the Lord created them from the dust of the earth

For the Lord created Adam from the red clay

For man and louse are brothers before the mercy seat

For he is called Smart for he smarts from the whips of his
    keepers

For he is called Christopher for he also is a bearer of Christ

Let Smart, house of Smart, rejoice with poor Jeoffrey, his
    good cat

For the cherub cat is a term of the angel tiger.

Kenneth Lillington

PROBLEM

The wind is in the north, the wind
Unfurls its fury at the door;
To turn the cat out seems unkind.

To use him ill I do abhor,
Yet this reflection comes to mind:
Suppose he desecrates the floor?

Though hateful what he'll leave behind,
(To cleanse which were a loathsome chore)
To turn the cat out seems unkind.

He eats a lot, and cries for more:
Roughage, alas, which does not bind:
Suppose he desecrates the floor?

But what if with the dawn I find
Him frozen stiff, and frosted o'er?
To turn the cat out seems unkind.

I'll leave my lino with a score
Of daily journals amply lined:
Suppose he desecrates the floor?
To turn the cat out seems unkind.

John Gallen

LINES ON THE DEATH OF A CAT

It is so important that my grief be not absurd.
Some part of me is under earth with the cat:
The black-and-white, the woman-looking cat—
(Children sob for dogs, dead aunts only frighten them)
This is the stammering sincerity of the humbled.

It is so important that you should not laugh—
Some life that loved me is sordidly ceased.
Me out of a world of betters this free warm thing
Sought me and me at every instant. Who now
Seeks so? None. I pray you do not smile:
For o it is so important my grief be not absurd.

Maurice Craig

HIGH ON A RIDGE OF TILES

High on a ridge of tiles
A cat, erect and lean,
Looks down and slyly smiles;
The pointed ears are keen,
Listening for a sound
To rise from the backyard.
He casts upon the ground
A moment's cold regard.

Whatever has occurred
Is on so small a scale
That we can but infer
From the trembling of the tail
And the look of blank surprise
That glares out of the eyes
That underneath black fur
His face is deathly pale.

Maurice Craig

THREE CAT POEMS

I
ADDRESS OF WELCOME

Like cattle-raiding heroes in the Táin
I've made a kitten-raid across the Boyne;
And you, who lately to your mother clung,
Have travelled far indeed for one so young.

II
OCCASION OF SIN

There's retribution in the Judgment Day
For all who've led an innocent astray.
Each time I leave the room I think of that,
And lock the butter out of reach of cat.

III
THE BOOK OF LIFE

Restored to favour, he's allowed to look
Over my shoulder while I read a book;
Some day, no doubt, I'll be no more than such
And lucky if I understand as much.

Fergus Allen

from 'OTHER'

I can believe in a world of vegetation,
Weather and mechanical insects, but flinch
When our black cat, *Felis catus*, stands revealed
As a foreign body elbow deep in meadow,
Weighing me up with his incurious eyes—
The slits of an armoured car would show more interest.

This is the familiar that an hour ago
Flatteringly weaved and purred around my ankles;
Now, among buttercups and timothy-grass,
He might have descended from a flying saucer—
Alien as the peacock on our bathroom roof
Screaming challenges from the time of the dinosaurs.

Michael Hamburger

LONDON TOM-CAT

Look at the gentle savage, monstrous gentleman
With jungles in his heart, yet metropolitan
As we shall never be; who—while his human hosts,
Afraid of their own past and its primaeval ghosts,
Pile up great walls for comfort—walks coquettishly
Through their elaborate cares, sure of himself and free
To be like them, domesticated, or aloof!
A dandy in the room, a demon on the roof,
He's delicately tough, endearingly reserved,
Adaptable, fastidious, rope-and-fibre nerved.
Now an accomplished Yogi good at sitting still
He ponders ancient mysteries on the window-sill,
Now stretches, bares his claws and saunters off to find
The thrills of love and hunting, cunningly combined.
Acrobat, diplomat, and simple tabby-cat,
He conjures tangled forests in a furnished flat.

U.A. Fanthorpe

ODYSSEUS' CAT

Aged and broken, prostrate on the ground,
Neglected Argus lies, once fabled hound.
Odysseus' footsteps he alone descries,
Perceives the master through the slave's disguise;
He lifts his head, and wags his tail, and dies.
                    —*The Corgiad*, trans. J.G.C.

                    Not that I don't believe
The first part of the yarn—the ten years' war.
Ten seems quite modest for a genocide.
No, it's the ten years' journey afterwards
I boggle at, bearing in mind
The undemanding nature of the route.
Why did he take so long? One thing's for sure—
Those junkies, cannibals, one-eyed aliens,
And friendly ladies living alone on islands—
Well, what do you think? Of course. Exactly.

In the meantime, in another part of the archipelago,
Old Argus had been catsmeat long before.
Man's best wears out, with rushing around and barking,
And digging and wagging. Cats, on the contrary, last:
The harmonious posture, exact napping,
Judicious absences from home ...
                    I had, of course,
Been busy. Did what I could to discourage
The mistress's unappealing Don Juans,
Lurked boldly in dark corners, slashing
Shins of passers-by; performed
Uninhibited glissades down dinner tables,
Scattering wine and olives; free fell
From rafters upon undefended necks;

Produced well-timed vomit in my lady's chamber
When a gallant went too far; and I helped
With demolishing the tapestry each night,
Having an inbred talent.

So when Odysseus came, I rubbed his legs.
He recognized me—well, he said, *Puss, puss,*
Which is all you learn to expect.
                            And then the liar
Concocts this monstrous calumny of me:
He leaves me out, supplants me with a dog,
A dead dog, too, And the one thing
Everyone believes is that dog's tale,
Tale of the faithful hound.
                            You'll see
I've improved his version; cut out the lies,
The sex, the violence. Poor old Argus
Wouldn't have known the difference. But cats
Are civilized. I thought you'd see it my way.

Thom Gunn

APARTMENT CATS

The Girls wake, stretch, and pad up to the door.
  They rub my leg and purr:
  One sniffs around my shoe,
  Rich with an outside smell,
 The other rolls back on the floor—
White bib exposed, and stomach of soft fur.

Now, more awake, they re-enact Ben Hur
  Along the corridor,
  Wheel, gallop; as they do,
  Their noses twitching still,
 Their eyes get wild, their bodies tense,
Their usual prudence seemingly withdraws.

And then they wrestle: parry, lock of paws,
  Blind hug of close defence,
  Tail-thump, and smothered mew.
  If either, though, feels claws,
 She abruptly rises, knowing well
How to stalk off in wise indifference.

Ted Hughes

ESTHER'S TOMCAT

Daylong this tomcat lies stretched flat
As an old rough mat, no mouth and no eyes.
Continual wars and wives are what
Have tattered his ears and battered his head.

Like a bundle of old rope and iron
Sleeps till blue dusk. Then reappear
His eyes, green as ringstones; he yawns wide red,
Fangs fine as a lady's needle and bright.

A tomcat sprang at a mounted knight,
Locked round his neck like a trap of hooks
While the knight rode fighting its clawing and bite.
After hundreds of years the stain's there

On the stone where he fell, dead of the tom:
That was at Barnborough. The tomcat still
Grallochs odd dogs on the quiet,
Will take the head clean off your simple pullet,

Is unkillable. From the dog's fury,
From gunshot fired point-blank he brings
His skin whole, and whole
From owlish moons and bekittenings

Among ashcans. He leaps and lightly
Walks upon sleep, his mind on the moon.
Nightly over the round world of men
Over the roofs go his eyes and outcry.

Ted Hughes

OF CATS

A heart constituted wholly of cats
(Even as the family nose derives)
From father and mother a child inherits,
And every cat gets fully nine lives.

Wildest cats, with scruff cats, queenly cats
(Crowned), they jig to violins; they go stately
Where a torched pageantry celebrates
A burial, or crowning (of a cat); or sing sweetly.

At your ears and in harmony left with right
Till the moon bemoods: to the new, to the full,
Only look up: possessing night—
Cattic Bacchanal! A world of wild lamps and wauling,

A world gone to the cats, every cat of the heart out,
And darkness and light a cat upon a cat—.
They have outwitted our nimblest wits.
One who, one night, sank a cat in a sack

With a stone to the canal-bottom
 (Under the bridge, in the very belly of the black)
And hurried a mile home
Found that cat on the doorstep waiting for him.

So are we all held in utter mock by the cats.

Jon Silkin

HIS CAT

Fifteen and adult, I lift our tortoise-hue cat
to a glass box, a doctor's phial twisting in mud-green vapor,
and like a kid a winter's sigh comes at mother's 'Gas her.'
Doctor asks, 'Will you stay and watch?' Am I afraid?
She raises her docile head and smiling fangs, asking
'Cease killing me.' She looks, and then she dies.

I flee to the priest his mouth dabbed with angel cake:
'But child, she has gone into the world of light,'
where, under the church's arch—O, hell, O divine
promise—I find no mercy for for myself or her.
My failed self and a gassed animal.
The arch is an arrowless bow, wanting desire.
Here's where I stand.

In my palm is a mute bell, her name,
a collar, some tangled hairs. Stood on a railway cutting,
do I suppose grass restores? No suicide,
still, I trespass across the electrification
and reach the station's bridge-form, 1864.
This war takes boys to France with makeshift steam,
the schedules cramming the morring-place by London Bridge,
the soldier-killers heaped in tears, the carriages
like coffins, flickering over rails to the horizon of battle.
The destruction of the resistance to do it.
The jouissance at the gun's discharge of souls at each other.

Who are you to say I am too young to kill?
I had a cat nine inches tall, of indelible grace.
But the boys, the flag of their disposition,
Fragile, stained, aching flag. I, a child, succeed.

Blade upon blade of sacrifice, even of grass.
But will the creature forgive what I have done?

My father is not a soldier to praise or blame.
Nor is my God, though his church says that all may wear guns
and deliver gas shells into another's right to life.
When I stand at sentry, the voices of bird and cat
and breathless mule, and the sigh wrinkling past the septum
of the horse tethered to a stake;
I, having no less right to life,
hear that the mud is silent as earth's depths.

Roger McGough

MY CAT AND I

Girls are simply the prettiest things
My cat and i believe
And we're always saddened
When it's time for them to leave

We watch them titivating
(that often takes a while)
And though they keep us waiting
My cat & i just smile

We like to see them to the door
Say how sad it couldn't last
Then my cat and i go back inside
And talk about the past.

Michael Longley

TAM

was a Burmese tom whose ears
harked back to the fruit-eating bat
wide awake in the branches, wing-
membranes shading the feast;

whose whiskers hinted at otters
and a drink of water; whose paw
was a squirrel's paw with monkey
finger-pads; whose shoulder-blades,

even when he was old, allowed
a kangaroo's negotiation
of the rheumaticy staircase;
whose tail was entirely his own,

whose sex was a hazel-nut kernel,
whose blink a compression of primrose
petals or, for the sheen, celandine;
whose yodel conversed with owls,

whose purr with all of us under
the one roof; whose, name, coloured
by his trek across contintents
and the trade-routes, was Tamarind.

Derek Mahon

AUTUMN BLUES (after Mallarmé)

Ever since Maria left for another star—Orion perhaps; Altair; or you, green Venus?—I've been savouring my solitude. What long days I've spent alone with my cat. By 'alone' I mean, of course, 'without another material being', for a cat is a *mystical* presence, a spirit. So I can honestly say that I've spent long days alone with my cat, and alone too with one of the last authors of the Roman decadence; for, now that the fair creature is no more, I've been strangely enamoured of everything contained in the phrase 'decline and fall'. By the same token, my favourite time of year is the drawn-out end of summer immediately preceding autumn, and my favourite time of day, the time I set aside for my walk, that moment when the sun, before disappearing, throws a yellow copper light on the grey walls, a red copper light on the window-panes. Similarly, the sort of literature I now read for pleasure is that exquisite poetry from the last days of Rome—only, however, in so far as it breathes no hint of the barbarians' thrilling approach, much less starts babbling the early Christian authors' baby Latin

So there I was, reading one of those touching poems whose cosmetic finish is so much more pleasing than any youthful glow, one hand plunged in the fur of an innocent beast, when a barbarous barrel-organ started up slowly and mournfully under the window, playing to a long avenue of poplars whose leaves struck me as cheerless even in spring—ever since, in fact, Maria walked there last with her candelabrum. A music for the lonely, yes indeed. A piano twinkles, a fiddle-bow draws light from the riven strings; but the barrel-organ, in this reminiscential dusk, set me desperately dreaming. And while it murmured a hackneyed, cheerfully popular tune, introducing some sort of gaiety to the neighbourhood, I asked myself why this trite refrain should touch me so to the quick, like a romantic ballad, and bring tears to my eyes. I listened carefully but flung no coin from the window—not wishing to change position, reluctant to notice that the instrument was not the only singer.

Eiléan Ní Chuillenáin

CYPHER

My black cat lies still,
Washed, in the third of her lives
Veteran squatter, *porte-malheur*, she survives
Absorbing light on the sill.

While I wipe and scour,
Polish the glasses grimly,
The pard-shadow of the high crooked chimney
Slips closer by the hour.

What man forgets, at home
In the long noons of peace
His own imprisonment or the day of his release?
Could I forget this room

This view, the cleaning habit
All shared with Pussy?
Forsan et haec olim meminisse
Juvabit.

Thomas Lynch

GRIMALKIN

One of these days she will lie there and be dead.
I'll take her out back in a garbage bag
and bury her among my son's canaries,
the ill-fated turtles, a pair of angelfish:
the tragic and mannerly household pests
that had the better sense to take their leaves
before their welcomes or my patience had worn thin.
For twelve long years I've suffered this damned cat
while Mike, my darling middle-son, himself
twelve years this coming May, has grown into
the tender if quick-tempered manchild
his breeding blessed and cursed him to become.
And only his affection keeps this cat alive
though more than once I've threatened violence—
the brick and burlap in the river recompense
for mounds of furballs littering the house,
choking the vacuum cleaner, or what's worse:
shit in the closets, piss in the planters, mice
that winter indoors safely as she sleeps
curled about a table-leg, vigilant
as any knick-knack in a partial coma.
But Mike, of course, is blind to all of it—
the grey angora breed of arrogance,
the sluttish roar, the way she disappears for days
sex-desperate once or twice a year,
urgently ripping her way out the screen door
to have her way with anything that moves
while Mike sits up with tuna fish and worry,
crying into the darkness 'here kitty kitty',
mindless of her whorish treacheries;
or of her crimes against upholsteries—
the sofas, love seats, wingbacks, easychairs

she's puked and mauled into dilapidation.
I have this reoccurring dream of driving her
deep into the desert east of town
and dumping her out there with a few days feed
and water. In the dream, she's always found
by kindly tribespeople who eat her kind
on certain holy days as a form of penance.
God knows, I don't know what he sees in her.
Sometimes he holds her like a child in his arms
rubbing her underside until she sounds
like one of those battery powered vibrators
folks claim to use for the ache in their shoulders.
And under Mike's protection she will fix her
indolent green-eyed gaze on me as if
to say: Whaddaya gonna do about it, Slick,
the child loves me and you love the child.
Truth told, I really ought to have her fixed
in the old way with an air-tight alibi,
a bag of ready-mix and no eyewitnesses.

But one of these days she will lie there and be dead.
And choking back loud hallelujahs, I'll pretend
a brief bereavement for my Michael's sake,
letting him think as he often said
'deep down inside you really love her don't you Dad.'
I'll even hold some cheerful obsequies
careful to observe God's never-failing care
for even these, the least of His creatures,
making some mention of cat-heaven where
cat-ashes to ashes, cat-dust to dust
and the Lord gives and the Lord has taken away.
Thus claiming my innocence to the end,
I'll turn Mike homeward from that wicked little grave
and if he asks, we'll get another one because
all boys need practice in the arts of love
and all boys' ageing fathers in the arts of rage.

Vikram Seth

THE STRAY CAT

The grey cat stirs upon the ledge
Outside the glass doors just at dawn.
I open it; he tries to wedge
His nose indoors. It is withdrawn.
He sits back to assess my mood.
He sees me frown; he thinks of food.

I am familiar with his stunts.
His Grace, unfed, will not expire.
He may be hungry, but he hunts
When need compels him, or desire.
Just yesterday he caught a mouse
And yoyoed it outside the house.

But now he turns his topaz eyes
Upon my eyes, which must reveal
The private pressures of these days,
The numb anxieties I feel.
But no, his greyness settles back
And yawns, and lets his limbs go slack.

He ventures forth an easy paw
As if in bargain. Thus addressed,
I fetch a bowl, and watch him gnaw
The star-shaped nuggets he likes best.
He is permitted food, and I
The furred indulgence of a sigh.

Anon

A CAT'S CONSCIENCE

A Dog will often steal a bone,
But conscience lets him not alone,
And by his tail his guilt is known.

But cats consider theft a game,
And, howsoever you may blame,
Refuse the slightest sign of shame.

When food mysteriously goes,
The chances are that Pussy knows
More than she leads you to suppose.

And hence there is no need for you,
If Puss declines a meal or two,
To feel her pulse and make ado.

INDEX